Roker Beach

Roker Beach

A boy and a bomb

Copyright © 2025 Geoff Pearson

All rights reserved

ISBN: 979-8-30552-410-9

Cats and Flies

It didn't have to be this way, none of this was planned. But then most families are not planned, not working towards a grand design, they just happen. Sometimes we might wish a different path had been taken, often we are following expectations of others, and only when looking back do we see what might have been.

This is a story of a family that grew through moments of unexpected and radical change. That these moments were happening was not apparent at the time. Only now, long after everyone involved is dead, can their dramatic effects be seen. The question of "how did we get here" took some exploration.

Tom was born into a world of turmoil, in which poverty was never far away, where a world war had happened – he might be reading about that turmoil in that newspaper on the front cover in 1932. He escaped to create, from scratch, a life of respect and success.

In the modern world telling such a story would be difficult – the records would not exist. But paper outlives the Cloud and the USB stick There is nothing to beat a paper document already a century old; seeing how it has yellowed, reflecting that it must have been held by so many people now gone, peering at what is lying in the corner of a photograph.

Cats and Flies

In this story there are glimpses: photographs, masonic records, school reports, letters, greetings cards, newspaper reports and notices, and more. There is even a sound recording from 1946.

This story is about opportunities, unexpected events and consequences. Much of it is seen through a fog, with possibilities glimpsed, shadows of the truth flickering, secrets and confidences and every family will recognise the reality of it all.

Tom said he lived by two rules:

> More flies caught by treacle than vinegar,

> There are more ways of killing a cat than sticking coke in its ears.

Let me explain…

Haar

The north-east coast of Britain, from Northumberland northwards, faces into the North Sea and has many beautiful beaches, wide golden sands, and rocky bays quite different to resorts on the south coast or the Mediterranean. It has glorious dawns; with huge landscapes of the sun rising and shining through the gap between the horizon and the cloud base.

Much of the history of Britain arises from this coast, from Shetland, Orkney and Caithness which became part of Britain in 1472, through Aberdeen, core of fishing and oil industries, passing the Kingdom of Fife and Edinburgh, capital of Scotland. The coast continues to Newcastle-upon-Tyne, and the industrial complexes of Sunderland and Yorkshire – a sequence of proudly independent cultures each having a strong connection to the sea.

The interaction between sea and land produces weather of all kinds. The weather can be wild, always vigorous, and has shaped life at the sea edge. The history of Britain contains much fog; Charles Dickens makes much of this in Great Expectations, and London smog was a direct result of smoke-filled streets.

But the east coast fogs are much more exciting. "Haar" is a cold, white fog that comes from the sea, very often after a warm, sunny day.

Haar

A golden evening can often be followed by a morning of glowing white air – with a shimmer of sun above – a gentle hint of a bright day to come. Haar is often associated with good prospects for the coming day.

I am Geoff, standing with my father Tom on the prom overlooking Roker Beach, on the northern side of the River Wear. "Roker" may come from "roke", an east Yorkshire word for sea fog, believed to derive from the Swedish röka, meaning smoke. Haar, or roke, is a feature of summers along the north-east coast of Britain.

Tom parked his new, two-tone red and grey, Ford Anglia estate. He was wearing the uniform of a decent sort of chap: "sports jacket and flannels". There was probably a Clydella small-check shirt, Munrospun woollen reddish tie and a "V-neck" pullover. That was what he always wore – in hot weather the jacket, tie and pullover might be left off. He smoked a pipe, which involved considerable ritual of cleaning the bowl and laying a fresh bolt of tobacco, or if time was short, Players Senior Service cigarettes, from a white push-up packet. Smoking paraphernalia seemed important. The visit was soon after my moving into long trousers, usually with a blue pullover. Clothes were not important.

We had driven from North Cheshire the night before, pausing en route in Durham. We stayed in a bed and breakfast place there, one bedroom and floral wallpaper. and after breakfast drove to Roker. We parked and walked towards the sea – I recognised that Tom knew the place well, and I presumed it must have

Haar

carried memories of sunny days on the beach that he wanted to share with his son – who would see it for the first time. Tom, my mother Phyll, my sister Jan and I had holidayed in Bournemouth and Swanage from 1955, staying in comfortable hotels, usually warm and lively. We always went on trips together – always with a sense of excitement – perhaps thinking of the way the King, George VI had talked warmly and protectively of his family as "we four".

This trip was different; it was Easter 1963. We had just come out of the coldest winter since 1740 – lasting two months; our snow man, built at the end of the Christmas school holiday lasted well into the spring. Tom was on a mission. He and I (then 13 years old) had travelled to Sunderland leaving Phyll and Jan in Lymm, a comfortable village in Cheshire, to which the family had moved in 1962. The purpose of the trip was not made clear but appeared to be a couple of days with me to meet Tom's family for the first time. It was unexplained why this would be the first time I had met a group of my closest relatives. It might be, could be, should be, a happy family reunion; Tom had probably not seen his family since his marriage to Phyll in 1945. Even so, Tom did not seem to be excited at the prospect of showing off his son to his family. I sensed the mood – there was to be no moment for getting to know everyone. This was my serious, business-like, father preparing for a difficult day.

For perhaps the first time, I was standing next to my father as a man, no longer a child and I could tell he was uncertain how this was done. Equally, I had begun to wonder what to call him; until then he had been "Daddy" which increasingly seemed childish

Haar

as we shifted into a new mode. He had always been affectionate, and was adored by us. He normally radiated a strong, very humorous, confident persona. He made friends easily – the life and soul of any social event, always interested but seldom open on his own thoughts and past.

Today, the beach at Roker was invisible. Even from the relatively low view point on the promenade we could see only just a few yards of sand – the beach was deeply swathed in haar, a cold, wet, muffled sound – the sea was barely audible even though the waves were lapping gently only 50 yards in front of us. The fog above us was bright as in the next few hours the sun might burn its way through the haar – it could turn out to be a bright but cold day.

The few moments at Roker did not lead Tom to explain why the trip was made now and without Phyll and Jan. Normally, I was irritatingly inquisitive, wanting to know, why, how and when about everything. This day there was no joking, not even an explanation of where we were. We had parked not far from his family and Tom was probably collecting his thoughts for the day ahead. It was not like those smart hotels in Bournemouth and Swanage in which we had holidayed in the 1950s. Roker seemed briefly to bring back happy memories of sunny days on the sands with his sisters and friends. But there was no excitement, no anticipation, for this visit and certainly no declared purpose. Little was said and I was nervous about meeting a whole new section of family, previously hardly mentioned.

Haar

Some years earlier, returning from one of our regular visits to Phyll's family in London, I had asked Tom if he had a grandfather – this did not bring much information. "Yes, his name was Miles Abstemious Pearson". Lightening the mood, Tom continued to explain that there was another Miles and he suggested, glumly, that he was called Miles Obadiah Pearson. He joked about Miles' mother using these full names when calling the boys in from play for their tea. But there the relating of family history ended. Much later I found that Miles Abstemious was the patriarch of the family but there was no one called Obadiah. There have been several Miles Pearsons, almost all close relatives.

Tom was the youngest of four children to James Edgar Pearson (called Jim) and Hannah Isabella Price, who had married in 1910 in Sunderland. Their first child was James Arnett, always called Arnett (it was the surname of James Edgar's mother) - born in 1911. The second child was Eileen May – born in 1915. Both Arnett and Eileen had albinism, with colourless complexions, white hair and pink eyes, which gave poor eyesight. This must have been a shock to their parents and with two in the family, there was a strong likelihood that this was inherited from previous generations. I don't think Tom mentioned this to me. The next child, Margarita Amy, was born in February 1920 and named after Hannah's sister, Margaretta, who had died in 1915. Finally, Thomas Wilfred came along on 8 September 1922; Wilfred was a name used several times in the Pearson pedigree. The signs suggested a close family.

Haar

There are village suburbs of Sunderland, like Ryhope and New Silksworth, built along many narrow streets of single storey terraced dwellings, some with a habitable roof space, with two rooms and an outside toilet in the yard behind. Sunderland had been created by the amalgamation of three settlements on either side of the River Wear and had become a major centre of iron, coal and ship-building. There were "new towns" built by the mining companies for coal workers and their families in the late nineteenth century. Miners had come from all over Britain, including from other such communities; and it might be that a new house was part of the attraction. There had to be some incentive beyond avoiding unemployment and deep poverty. But by the 1960s these streets were far from bijou dwellings.

Father and son returned to the car and drove to meet the present family. The sun cleared the haar to reveal streets of houses unlike anything I had seen before.

In Cheshire we lived in a large 4 bedroom detached house, with central heating, a kitchen with adjoining laundry and pantry, surrounded by gardens overlooking fields. The car would be parked on the drive before being put away in the garage. Our dachshund would romp in the garden.

We had moved to Lymm in Cheshire in April 1962, a country village less than 30 miles from Salford, a town which was the location for Coronation Street, a twice-weekly "gritty" TV soap. Those grainy, black and white, TV images of the terraced houses and the apparently rough lives of the families which populated the "Street" now seemed to be alive in Sunderland.

Haar

Today, these Sunderland houses are extensively refurbished and modernised but still at heart tiny homes. In 1962 that process had not begun; Amy lived in Hedley Terrace, married to Jimmy Gibson. Jimmy had been married before but his wife, Louise, had died and their son, Alan, was grown up.

Eileen had married and moved to London and Arnett had a "corner" shop in Milburn Street in Sunderland. The days here are blurred in my mind; there was a warm welcome from Amy with home cooking in a warm but cramped house. Arnett was seen and we were greeted, gruffly, in the street.

These were people I did not know, who lived in a community quite different to any of my experience. I had become used to the north-western accent of Lymm (but never acquired it) but here were my own blood relatives with an even trickier accent – then called Geordie, now spoken of as Mackem. Tom no longer had that accent – a recording exists of a 1946 Christmas message in which he uses a very patrician, almost strangulated, style. On this visit he struggled to regain something of his former accent with phrases "why aye hinny"– conscious of the risk of sounding aloof.

At some point Tom slipped away for the real business of the visit, which did not become apparent until many decades later. I was left with Amy in a tiny house, warm with a strong smell of apple pie home baking. She was friendly, with sparkling eyes and deeply black hair, and fascinating in that she knew Tom well (she was only 2 and a half years older than him). Amy and Tom were born after the First War, whereas Arnett and Eileen came before. It was almost two separate families. Arnett and Eileen seemed distant, whereas Amy, almost the same age as my mother, was engaging.

Tom came back from his meeting and there was light, almost incomprehensible, talk as he was brought up to date on local and family matters. Later that April day, Tom and I drove to see James Edgar Pearson, the head of the family, then aged 78, who lived in modern, sheltered housing in Rhondda Road, East Herrington, with Harriet Curran. Tom's mother, Hannah Isabella, had died in 1943. By 1963, Jim was in a wheelchair but able to work in the small garden that went with the house. Harriet pushed him into the back garden so we might see the potatoes which he tended with long-handled implements. In a magazine rack at the side of his chair he kept, as many older people do, death notices and obituaries from which he gave us a running tally of deaths of people that he and, perhaps, Tom had known. His broad accent was so strong that I could not understood what was said and Tom had to interpret, while my terrified replies to questions had to be repeated in a stronger voice by Tom. There was no explanation of who Harriet night be. She did not sit with us nor engage in chatter; it is hard to recall this as a warm encounter and we did not stay long. There was an evident contrast between this and the lively, affectionate way in which family banter occurred between Tom and Phyll's family. Laughter and teasing were Tom's key tools with us.

We drove home later that day to our centrally-heated, detached house with 4 bedrooms, a sitting room with inglenook, a dining room, bathroom, kitchen, scullery, garage, all surrounded by our

Haar

gardens and open fields. I returned to my grammar school education, Jan went to a private school in Altrincham. Phyll had a dachshund and a person to help with housework. Sunderland was not mentioned much.

Even so, James Edgar and Harriet came to visit us in Lymm for a few days in 1965 – collected from Sunderland by Tom by car. Jim died in December 1966 (I'm not sure if Tom attended the funeral) and Harriet in 1974, both in Sunderland.

We saw the Sunderland family only once more.

Hannah Isabel,   Eileen May,   [Unknown],   (Margarita) Amy

Amy Vida,   James Edgar,   Thomas Wilfred

Borrowby to Bishopwearmouth

Amy Vida at Tan Cottage, Borrowby

Borrowby to Bishopwearmouth

The Pearson family first appears around 1700 in Kirby Malham, in north Yorkshire, working with sheep and the name Miles appears in most subsequent generations. By 1820 Miles Pearson was a tanner living at Tan Cottage (which still exists) in Borrowby. His son, Wilfred Sadler Pearson, continued the wool association by becoming a master tailor, still in Borrowby. In 1841, Wilfred was married in Leake Church to Mary Kirk, a dressmaker, by whom he had 8 children. Leake is a hamlet dating from the times of the Domesday book but now has a population of only around 10 persons. Borrowby is in the parish of Leake Its size and surroundings imply a grander past and there are many memorials to Pearson, Kirk and other local families.

In the graveyard of Leake Church there are stones recording the deaths of 4 of the eight Pearson children, all in one week in April 1860. They had died day by day of diphtheria in one of the several epidemics of the time. Mary's brother was the stonemason for Leake and will have made the gravestones for his nieces and nephews. Two other daughters had already left home to marry, another had died at birth, leaving only Miles Abstemious Pearson to carry forward the name.

How an infant came to be named Abstemious is a puzzle. It might have reflected the rise of Primitive Methodism: there was such a chapel in Borrowby but there was no continuing family religious fervour. It seems likely that this is the only recorded use of that name – quite an asset when searching records.

Borrowby to Bishopwearmouth

Miles became apprenticed as a tailor to his father at 19 years of age.

For centuries, the area had centred on Northallerton, an ancient market town and on the main coaching routes north and south from North Yorkshire and just 5 miles or so away.

Gradually the family looked northwards to Sunderland the growing industrial centre which had absorbed the villages of Bishopwearmouth and Monkwearmouth (on the opposite bank of the River Wear). Iron and coal were bringing prosperity to the north-east, benefitting Sunderland. For Miles Abstemious, the obvious future was there. Travel to Sunderland was easy, trains ran from Northallerton. Trips like that became frequent to buy tailoring and drapery materials from a supplier in 62 Brougham Street, where he first met Lydia Mary Arnett and married her in 1873.

Lydia Mary Arnett brought several new features to the family. She came from East Harlsey, just 4 miles north of Borrowby, a centre of flax (and so linen) production. Her father was George Arnett (1816-1887) – who is first seen in the records as a hosier (stockings and the like) and later was described as a stationer (despite being unable to write – his marriage certificate is signed "his mark"). The records show him managing a hosiery shop at 291 High Street, Bishopwearmouth – with no clear explanation of how that came about.

By comparing street directories and family records, there are signs, hard to prove, that he had worked in a hosier's shop at

Borrowby to Bishopwearmouth

22 High Street West in Bishopwearmouth, owned by a man called Calvert. One surmise is that Calvert died and George married his young widow, Emma (or Amy) Beaver (1815-1877), who came from Stibbington in Northamptonshire. At the time of their marriage, Emma lived at 23 High Street West, Bishopwearmouth. In due course, she died in 1887 at 14½ Villiers Street, later also the home of Miles Abstemious.

Meanwhile, on Saturday 11 August 1888, the Pearson family house contents in Borrowby were advertised for sale by auction under instruction from Miles Pearson (presumably Miles Abstemious). The house, Tan Cottage, was probably rented, as was common, almost normal, at the time. By 1891, Wilfred is 77 years old and living in Whitley Minor, north of Sunderland, with his daughter Sarah who had married Robert Mason, a foreman tanner. Wilfred is a "retired tailor" and working in a tannery, presumably under Robert.

In 1890, Miles Abstemious was living at 11 Kensington Terrace, Sunderland, working as a draper's assistant, but nipped back to Borrowby in April 1893 for the birth of his only daughter, Amy Vida. He died in Borrowby in 1929, living at Fern House and described as a "Gentleman". By then, life in Borrowby had ended for all the family. Miles' sons had moved to Hull, Islington and Brighton and may well have little contact with each other.

James Edgar (for whom there is no record of his birth on 5 November 1884) first appears in 1901 living at 1 Offerton Street, Sunderland, a property his mother Lydia Mary had brought into

Borrowby to Bishopwearmouth

the family. He is working as a joiner. In 1911 he is living at 15 Hemming Street, Grangetown, Sunderland where he is a shop assistant; he had married Hannah Isabella Price in St Mark's Church, Millfield, Sunderland on 4 December 1910 and she is with him in Hemming Street.

Hannah's family had come from Northumberland and Suffolk; her grandfather William Vince had been a steamboat master and ran the Blyth lifeboat. His family had sailed up from Norfolk through the 19th century – he married Eleanor Burn, from Bedlington. Her mother, Rebecca Burn Vince, combined the surnames as did her uncle Robinson Burn Vince. In 1891, Hannah was living with uncle Robinson and his wife, rather than at home, suggesting a close family. Hannah's sister Margaretta lived in Castle Ward, Northumberland and Tom's sister Amy was formally christened Margarita Amy. Rebecca Burn Vince lived until 1938, perhaps in Borrowby.

It is hard to tell how much of this was known to Tom, confined to the claustrophobia of Sunderland and Ryhope. His early years were spent in New Silksworth and Ryhope surrounded by many narrow streets of single storey terraced houses. When James Edgar had his butcher's business at 18 Ryhope Street South, the family lived over the shop with many photographs taken in the yard. Tom said that James Edgar did his own slaughtering of livestock in that yard; hard to imagine today. The business supported a car, a Bullnose Morris, a van, a cart and horse and the household had a maid.

Borrowby to Bishopwearmouth

Messrs. E. & J. PETERS,
Solicitors, 4, New Street, York.

BORROWBY, NEAR THIRSK.

MESSRS. ROBINSON AND HARLAND Beg to announce their instructions from Mr. MILES PEARSON, to SELL BY AUCTION, at Borrowby aforesaid, on SATURDAY, August 11th, 1883, the whole of his HOUSEHOLD FURNITURE, &c., viz.:—

BEDROOMS.

BEDROOM No. 1.—Mahogany Four-post Bedstead and Bedding, Dressing Table, Washstand, Towel Rail, Commode, Wardrobe, Chest of Drawers, Toilet Glass, Mahogany Chest of Drawers, Carpet, Hearthrug, Toilet Covers, Timepiece, Pictures, Chamber Ware, &c.

BEDROOM No. 2.—Half-tester Bedstead and hangings, Bedding, Mattress, Dressing Table, Washstand, Round Table, Mahogany Chest of Drawers, Four Chairs, Toilet Glass, Chamber Ware, Window Curtains and Fringe, Carpet and Hearthrug, Pictures, Ornaments, Two Iron Bedsteads, Mattresses, Child's Crib, &c.

DRAWING ROOM.

Mahogany Centre Table, Gent's Mahogany Arm Chair, Six Mahogany Small Chairs, Mahogany Sofa, Piano (by Sherbrooke, London), Stand Table, Centre Table, Chimney Glass, Glass Bookcase in rosewood, Cornice Pole and Ring, Eight days' Clock in Mahogany case, Pedestal Clock, Steel mounted Fender and Irons, Ash Pan, Coal Vase, Spitoon, Two Reading Lamps, Paraffin Lamp, Carpet and Hearthrug, Table Cloth, etc.

KITCHEN.

Two Deal Tables with drawers, Sofa, Folding Table in rosewood, Three Windsor Chairs, Arm Chair, Press and Four drawers, Press and Three Drawers, Stools, Window Stand, Wringing Machine, Timepiece, Fire Tidy, Fire Guard, Washing Tubs, Flour Bin, Pictures, Ornaments, Pots, Pans, and the usual Crockery, &c.

SUNDRIES.

Long Traces, Horse Collar, Shovels, Spades, Brushes, Crowbar, Wheelbarrow, Two Ladders, Barrels, Boxes, Two Pig Troughs, Waterproof Knee Rug, Hampers, Pair Cart Wheels, Springs and Axletrees, quantity of Cow Chains, &c.

Sale to commence at ONE o'clock.
The Auctioneers invite prompt attendance.
Offices:—Northallerton, and Thirsk.

Borrowby to Bishopwearmouth

New Silksworth 1932

Amy Vida

Amy Vida

Tom's aunt Amy Vida was the last child of Miles Abstemious Pearson, born in 1893, almost 20 years after the first child, Frederick Ernest. In 1911, she was an apprentice dressmaker, probably taking after her parents who were variously drapers and tailors. In 1916 she married Richard Webb whose father was an "assurance" agent, and the family lived at 154 Cleveland Road a (relatively) smart terrace of 2 storey houses, albeit surrounded by the classic Sunderland single storey terrace cottages. Richard's father, John George Webb, was born in Calcutta; Richard was the first of 5 children and in 1911 was an Engineer Clerk. It looks as though the family would be well-off but by 1919 John was dead – leaving an estate of £629 to his widow.

Richard Webb joined the Royal Navy on 30 October 1916 at HMS Victory II, a shore establishment, as a "seagoing engineer (fitter)". He was demobbed from the Navy on 25 June 1919 and paid a War Gratuity of £257 on 2 March 1931. In 1921, he and Amy Vida were living with his mother, siblings and boarders at Cleveland Road. He is shown as a "Waterman, on his own account, on the River Wear". Then in 1922 Richard's mother died – presumably the household at 154 Cleveland Road was then broken up. His brothers and sister were in office jobs – not much like a "Wear waterman". On 6 February 1925 he embarked at Southampton for Buenos Aires as a member of the

Amy Vida

crew of the passenger liner "Almanzora". The trail of Richard ends here. He does not reappear.

There could be more: the "Windrush" is commonly believed to be the first boat to have brought post-war migrants from the Caribbean to Britain in 1948. The ship's arrival has been commemorated in hundreds of public accounts, and the name Windrush has become symbolic of the generation of Caribbean people who arrived in Britain during this period. But far less is known about the two ships that arrived before the Windrush, carrying smaller but still significant numbers of migrants: the S.S. Ormonde, which docked in Liverpool in March 1947, carrying 108 passengers, and the Almanzora, carrying around 200 passengers, which arrived in December of the same year.

Perhaps Richard Webb continued a life at sea, perhaps he died, freeing Amy Vida.

Amy Vida

Back in Sunderland, matters take a natural turn. In the 1939 Register, taken to prepare the population for War, for issuing identity cards, Amy Vida is recorded as married to Thomas Launcelot Stott, Engine Fitter, Marine Engine Works, born 30 November 1890 – and they are living at 2 Ancona Street, Sunderland. Divorce from Richard Webb is unlikely and expensive. So Amy Vida was some kind of semi-widow, neither free nor bound, passing herself as married to Thomas Launcelot Stott. In 1915 Thomas Stott had married Emily Moffatt but she died the following year, no doubt in childbirth.

Then, in 1950, Thomas married "Amy V Webb" - properly. He is the same age as Richard would have been, within a couple of months, possibly workmates given their similar roles, or even friends. There were to be no children – so no harm is done.

Peter Clarke, Amy Vida's nephew, reported that she had scoliosis, a curvature of the spine, and there are photographs of her suggesting that it affected her quite early on. Amy Vida died in 1960 from "congestive heart failure accelerated by a fracture of right humerus due to a fall at her home". Peter suggested that she had, at one time, owned a number of houses in Ancona Street – if so, the canny business approach no doubt came from her mother, Lydia Mary Arnett and grandmother, Emma (Amy) Beaver.

Thomas Launcelot Stott inherited her estate. Just 2 years later, on 17 December 1962, he died having made his last Will and Testament on 3 April that year. The executor of the will was his nephew Thomas Wharton of 40 Ancona Street, just along from

Amy Vida

his and Amy Vida's home at No 2. The estate totalled £1066 and 16 shillings net and was divided into 5 shares:

A quarter each to:

> Thomas Wharton,
>
> Arnett Pearson,
>
> Eileen Andersen (now divorced from Sam Clarke and married to Jens Andersen).

An eighth each to:

> Amy Gibson   (so Tom's siblings shared, albeit not equally)
>
> Harriet Curran.

Harriet was James Edgar's companion. By now they lived at 15 Rhondda Road. Tom's mother, Hannah Isabella, had died of cancer in 1943 and she may well have been very ill for some time, and needing help. Phyll described Harriet as James' "housekeeper". This may have been her role, and care-worker had been her employment when younger. It may be that she came into the life of the Pearsons around 1940 to help Hannah. However, after Hannah's death she was resident at Rhondda Road with James Edgar in a classic Council-provided old persons small bungalow and there was no income for them apart from the state pension. Given their age, it may just have been convenient to all that she move in. Perhaps the legacy went to her to avoid affecting James's income. She had two children,

Amy Vida

Ernest and Eva, who both married in 1941 leaving her free to look after James Edgar.

That visit to Sunderland in April 1963 was for the reading of the Stott Will.

The will makes no mention of Tom.

Tom would have thought it right to attend this clear landmark, regardless of his personal prospects. It is likely that he had not visited Sunderland for many years; he certainly took Phyll once after the War to meet his family; and his sisters and Peter Clarke, aged 7, had attended his wedding in 1945.

He never discussed his family. However, Gordon Stott, Thomas Stott's nephew, told me that he knew the Will had been an "issue".

Money is always a risky topic in families.

An Afternoon in the Sun

Chasing family history is a never-ending task; often a path falters, or peters out. The methodical assembly of history can be a vast jigsaw puzzle where the number of pieces and the ultimate portrait is unknown. As with a jigsaw, the game has to be played by connecting pieces that fit together – knowing there will be gaps and hoping they can be filled. The endless sequence of birth, marriage and death has many branches and not all are formally recorded.

In 2003, 40 years after the trip in the haar, I began to assemble the Pearson tree, knowing almost nothing, as Tom very seldom talked about his close family. I had met Tom's elder sister Eileen but finding her in the records was difficult, then I remembered that somehow we heard that she had divorced Sam Clarke and married a man called Jens Kristian Andersen. Gradually I found Jens, who put me in touch with her son, Peter Lawrence Clarke. With each name a new twig goes on the tree. He was 10 years older than me. He had been at my parents' wedding in September 1945, aged 7, with his mother, Eileen and aunt (Margarita) Amy. The formal wedding photographs show them all clearly.

A few months later, Peter dropped in to my home in Edinburgh, en route from his home in Rickmansworth to Aberdeen. We sat in the garden, making small talk – rather awkward as we had

An Afternoon in the Sun

never met before. All was well until he suggested that the family did not think that Tom was the son of James Edgar Pearson although Hannah Isabella Price was his wife and Tom's mother.

We chatted around this, with him asserting that "you'll never prove it". This should have been a surprise, even a shock, but with very little reflection this seemed to explain much. It fitted Tom's lack of interest in his family, far in style from his normal, warm approach. At that time, it seemed impossible to find a man, even then long dead, who might be the father of my father. There was no one left to provide the clues about a possibly brief event in late 1921. Nor was there anyone to suggest when the suspicion first emerged.

Tom never displayed family photographs – he may not have had any. I had not seen any from his family and knew them only from the 1963 flying visit; so Peter Clarke offered to lend me Eileen's photograph albums. He thought that she had been given a camera for her 16th birthday in September 1931. Over the next few years she took many photographs which record family and friends and these were held in two albums. This would have been a significant cost; the camera must have been a quality item; it took a small format film and most of the prints are small, possibly contact prints. Few were labelled. The albums and a family bible were returned to Peter in Rickmansworth some months later. However, I now had scans of all the photographs in Eileen's two albums and these have revealed much detail. Tom, Amy, Eileen and Arnett as well as Hannah and James Edgar are easy to spot. For many others that has been more difficult.

An Afternoon in the Sun

There are many photographs, starting from 1931, with a good number of Tom in boyish activities. The beaches, probably at Roker or Seaham, are popular; but even allowing for 1930s modesty most people are warmly dressed – North Sea breezes can be cutting. James Edgar had a backyard to his butcher shop, in New Silksworth, which is the scene of many: Tom about 10 or 11 years old sitting on his bike, Arnett, Eileen and Amy are young adults. There are no images of Tom as a teenager – perhaps because photography was expensive, and the 1930s were financially difficult. Arnett and Eileen stand out, often wearing sunglasses, very clearly albino with poor eyesight, white hair, and colourless eyes.

The arrival of reasonably-priced DNA testing and world-wide databases of the resulting DNA profiles might have identified new connections. I joined an early DNA sharing site, posting my DNA profile and waited for "matches". Quickly, I found matches with my mother's Dawkins family. I think the family were hoping for fame so I decided to ask Richard Dawkins, then holder of the Simonyi Professorship for the Public Understanding of Science at the University of Oxford to do a test which would be compared with that of my mother's brother Don. I sent him an email, one morning about 8am, within an hour he agreed, and the test was soon done. Don's was taken and we waited some weeks for the result.

There was no match, although Richard's result confirmed what he already knew as his family is listed in Burke's Peerage.

We are not gentry.

An Afternoon in the Sun

I then approached Phil Dawkins, owner of the Dawkins Genealogy website – we had not met but I had been able to help him extend his considerable database with material from my branch. We both did the DNA test and there was a match between us – it works! One Sunday morning he and I turned on our webcams – a novelty then – to find that we look like brothers and have many interests in common. Our common relative was Samuel Dawkins, 1763-1839. Samuel ended up with 18 children: five to a first wife and 13 to the second. Phil and I are both from the second wife. As we are so similar, this must mean that Samuel looked like us and proved that family traits can be enduring. In some, mysterious, way DNA carried forward more than just the basic physical structures. "Character" is an indefinable feature but mostly we do not start from scratch on that – children often "take after" one parent or the other. Phil and I had similar interests, not just family history, but places we had visited and more.

Did this mean that I could settle my father's paternity? I would have to find a male descendant of his grandfather and secure a test. With a fairly full family tree this should be easy. Miles Abstemious Pearson (1852-1929) had 4 sons: Frederick Ernest, Wilfred George, Arthur Miles and James Edgar. Wilfred had a son: Frank Miles who had been a sponsor at Tom's christening but he died, without children, in 1940. Arthur had left Borrowby by 1900 and became the head postmaster in Worthing.

Luckily it was easy to identify Frederick's son: Clifford, but he had died in 1980. Did he have a son? Was that son alive, where, and would he provide a DNA profile? This took quite a while to

An Afternoon in the Sun

unravel; but in 2008 I identified his son, John Frederick Pearson, just 10 years older than me. He lived near Doncaster, and responded to an email. The profile was taken and checked against mine.

If we were both descended from Miles Abstemious there should be a strong match, as between me and Phil Dawkins. But there was no match, and no thought in John's mind that his line had any "glitches". There was no one left to test to be sure that John Frederick's line was clear back to Miles Abstemious. As my line carried a sense of something not being right, it was more likely that that James Edgar was not my grandfather. His first two children, Arnett and Eileen, were clearly related: the albinism was obvious. The 1914-18 War intervened before my grandmother, Hannah Isabel Price, had her next child, the dark-haired (Margarita) Amy in February 1920 and finally Tom in September 1922.

At this stage, the family gossip runs out. If any one knew what had happened no one had said but perhaps the course I was following was wrong? Clearly, I was at a dead end unless I had another match. There was something, as why else would Peter Clarke raise it in our first and only meeting? One suggestion was that after two albino children (albeit two who seemed not to be much troubled by the condition), Hannah Isabella was determined to avoid another with that characteristic – although her third child, Amy, was fairly dark. That suggests some deliberate act, which seems almost malign, but there are faint hints of shenanigans.

An Afternoon in the Sun

Joining Ancestry.com, which includes a DNA register, quickly brought many matches with me from the Dawkins tribe. These are presented with an indicator of the likely distance of the relationship and as I have a comprehensive Dawkins database there are few surprises. There is a moderate DNA match with one of Amy's grandchildren but not strong enough to suggest that we share the same male line. It is much weaker than the equivalent matches with Dawkins (my mother's family) of similar generation separation. I am now in touch with cousins in Australia and New Zealand, descended from members of my maternal grandmother's family who had emigrated.

Then in 2019 a message appeared on Ancestry, from Sara, the wife of Alan Ferry, a new family name, with whom there was a close match. Sara set out some, mainly first, names but it was hard to see what the link might be. Late in 2023, I spent a weekend building a family tree for Alan who was a grandson of Thomas Taylor Ferry (the First), his father had been Thomas Taylor Ferry (the Second), son of the first. The Ferrys and Pearsons had lived close to each other – in the tight streets of Sunderland that was inevitable. Alan and Sara had moved to the south of England – I sent them the Ferry tree as I could see it. Almost by return, came the news that Alan's grandfather, Thomas Taylor Ferry (the First) was quite likely also to be my grandfather – it seemed not to be much of a surprise. Sara sent some photographs – including the wedding of Alan's father, Thomas Taylor Ferry (the Second) with Thomas Taylor Ferry (the First) at his side.

•

An Afternoon in the Sun

The resemblance between Thomas Taylor Ferry and my father is very evident. In fact, he looks much like me. Alan and I believe he and I are half cousins.

And how did this happen? Tom was born on 8 September 1922 – so what was happening on, say, Saturday 3 December 1921? Cardiff beat Sunderland 2:0? It would be the season of Christmas parties – probably not at home, as the houses were so small. Was this a party fling – a one-night stand or a longer clandestine liaison? Alan suggested that Thomas Taylor Ferry the First liked a good night out – he would routinely dress up and be out for an evening. In contrast, James Edgar seemed dour, perhaps depressed. Certainly Tom remembered touring the streets of Ryhope and Silksworth on the family cart and horse trying to persuade customers to pay their bills.

Thomas Taylor Ferry lived at 193 Cheltenham Road, just along the road from where Amy Vida had started her marriage with Richard Webb. The Ferrys and Pearsons could easily have known each other. Quite probably Thomas Taylor was a member of the Freemasons Lodge along with James Edgar. In July 1923 he and his wife had their fourth child, a son also called Thomas Taylor Ferry (the Second). Had Hannah Isabel named our Tom after his real father – so he produced two sons in a year, both called Thomas or Tommy (a name that the Pearsons had not used before)?

Did the family know? Is this why Tom was not mentioned in the Stott Will?

An Afternoon in the Sun

Perhaps Amy was also a Ferry child, and this why she received only a 1/8th share in the Will? But that would imply an affair extending over some years which would have been difficult to maintain in secret. Equally, was Tom the result of a one night stand and James Edgar oblivious to the reason for the family being extended? By the time of Eileen's albums, Tom was beyond the age of sitting on his Dad's knee.

Eileen's 1932 photo albums contain many group photographs, mainly with Hannah and James Edgar widely separated: frequently she is standing, with others, at the end of the back row, with James seated in the front row, next to quite elegant ladies, laughing. They show James Edgar and Arnett in front of the butchers shop at 18 Ryhope Street South. Ryhope, and several of the van proudly emblazoned with the name. There are many with James Edgar with other people, but very few of James and Hannah together. There are plenty of photos of Eileen and Amy arm in arm with their father; Tom is in some of these, but never alongside his mother.

But at some point, the butcher's business failed. James Edgar was made bankrupt and he became the Steward of the Conservative Club, 110 Hylton Road, Sunderland. Arnett joined him as a barman, and the whole family moved into the Club.

There is one group photo with Tom linking arms with James Edgar but James' attention is elsewhere. There are no photographs of Tom with his mother. This could be over-analysing but it is hard to avoid seeing indications that all was not well at home.

An Afternoon in the Sun

Tom's School Days

I said I would explain Tom's two rules:

"There are more ways of killing cats than sticking coke in their ears".

"Coke" was a solid fuel produced from coal. It had a gritty, pumice-like, texture, unlike coal which often had shiny, smooth surface. Basically this rule advised seeking simple rather than complicated solutions to problems.

"More flies caught by treacle than vinegar"

This seems to come from Benjamin Franklin's "Poor Richard's Almanac" in 1744, although Tom is unlikely to have read that. Taking a warm, friendly approach achieves more than confrontation.

He might have added *"strike while the iron is hot"*. He soon caught on to seizing opportunities – which were yet to come.

These rules provided his approach to all problems.

Ryhope Secondary School opened for 74 boys and 81 girls from 16 September 1911, but from 1929, the number of girls attending declined through the opening of nearby Seaham Girls Grammar and in 1933, Ryhope became an all-boys school. Tom entered on 11 September 1934 in the Autumn term, three days

Tom's School Days

after his 12th birthday. There are no more family photographs of Tom – no smiling parents showing off the new school uniform, no larking about on Roker Beach, no class of 1935. All we have are his school report books.

His first end of term report is summarised as "Pleasing Progress" by the Headmaster, Ralph G Williams. The subjects studied were:

> English (literature and composition),
> Geography,
> History,
> French,
> Mathematics (arithmetic, algebra, geometry),
> Science (chemistry, physics, biology),
> Drawing,
> Physical Exercises

He was 16th in the form, 1B. In the next term, he made "very creditable improvement" and, despite 24 days of absence, was 7th= in the form. The 1B year ended describing Tom as "a sound reliable worker" landing as 10th in the form. The term reports for 1935-36 were mainly "Good" and Very Good" supporting a position 8th in the form. In the year ending at Christmas 1936, the final summary is "He should be capable of passing into School Certificate form next year". In 1937 History was his top subject (highest mark in the class) with English "Very promising" – and was 5th in class.

Mr Williams reported "Splendid Progress".

Tom's School Days

King Lear

At school, Tom read "The Tragedy of King Lear" by William Shakespeare; reading such plays was a key part of a grammar school education. I have his copy, signed in the front and annotated and underlined throughout by him in ink. It is a bound edition, with sections sewn together. Like all Shakespeare, the story is complex – part of the reason for studying it is to unravel meaning – there can be many.

Basically, it begins as the Earl of Gloucester introduces his illegitimate son, Edgar, to the Earl of Kent. Lear, King of Britain, enters with his court. Now that he is an old man, Lear has decided to divide his kingdom between his three daughters. The division will depend on the quality of each princess' declarations of love for her father before the court. One daughter has rejected her father. So the future of four children is to be settled.

Almost every page of Tom's copy has his annotations and emphases – the book is well-used. Even so, when left open it does not lie flat except it falls open, naturally, at one page spread and only that one. Here, Tom has underlined, in ink, three lines uttered by Lear:

> "Nothing will come of nothing"

Then:

> "Here I disclaim all my parental care"

And further down the page:

> "As thou my sometime daughter"

Tom's School Days

By this time Tom seems to know that his mother's husband is not his father and is mature enough to read his own situation through Shakespeare's lines.

Arnett and Eileen were born just before the 1914-18 war. In a way, Tom and Amy were a second family, born after the war. James Edgar did not go to war, perhaps because he was involved in supply of food, as a butcher. It is easy to describe Tom's teenage years just as the youngest child in the family. However, these were not ordinary years.

The British Broadcasting Corporation had started in 1922, the year he was born and quickly became an essential of daily life. The news was given in rigorous terms, unfiltered by press barons in their newspapers. A world recession ran from 1929 to 1933 but the British economy struggled through the 1930s. The Great Depression of the 1930s was deeply felt in the north east – particularly with the collapse of shipbuilding in Jarrow. On Monday 5 October 1936 the Jarrow March set off on its first day of marching, 12 miles skirting round Sunderland to pause overnight at Chester-Le-Street. By 8 October, it had reached Northallerton before continuing to arrive at Marble Arch in London on 31 October. Tom must have been fully aware of this; the Depression was deeply felt by everyone in Sunderland.

At the same time, Germany, subdued after the First War, revived under Adolf Hitler, who became Führer in 1934, dominated world life until 1945. For a while, Hitler was able to persuade the world that he offered a recovery from economic depression but by 1935 he was riding rough-shod over the restrictions

Tom's School Days

placed on Germany following the end of the War. The expansion of his ambitions began to be explicit in 1936 but the world was slow to understand what was afoot and to act.

This formed the background to life for everyone in Britain.

Tom left Ryhope Secondary School in 1937 (aged 15) with the Head Teacher again reporting "Splendid Progress!". and in September he enrolled at Sunderland Bede Collegiate Boys' School – for which fees were paid each term to the Corporation of Sunderland. Bede was a school with a strong reputation and the family should have been proud of Tom's achievement in securing a place there. In 1938 the size of the school was significantly increased with the opening of new extensions, including a new physics laboratory, a new library and two new gymnasiums. In 1938 too, he gained the "School Certificate Awarded by the University of Oxford" in Form Upper V(A) and entered the Lower VI Form in the autumn.

Already Britain and its allies were preparing to take on Nazi Germany. Evacuation plans had been in preparation well before the outbreak of war. Small-scale evacuations of women and children were carried out in September 1938 but the real evacuation began in September 1939. The government had planned to evacuate about three million people but in the end only one million left home.

War was declared on Sunday 3 September 1939 after a summer of menace from Germany. Preparations had been underway for many months. On Sunday 10 September, two days after Tom's

Tom's School Days

17th birthday, the whole of the Bede Collegiate School was evacuated to Northallerton because industrial, ship-building Sunderland was expected to be a key target. 450 pupils were sent to share Northallerton Grammar School – in a "Cox and Box" arrangement – one school in the morning, the other in the afternoon. On 29 September 1939, the day when the 1939 Register was taken to provide data for National Identity Cards and ration books, Tom is recorded as "at school" and lodging in 8 Beaconsfield Road, Northallerton, with two other young men, fellow students. The lodging was with Ernest and Isabella Lightfoot; Ernest was a "Bricklayer's Labourer – Heavy Work" – they seem to have had no children. The whole school must have been accommodated in a similar way.

At Easter 1940 the Bede school reopened in Sunderland for the benefit of those pupils who had not been evacuated and by September 1940 most of the pupils had returned.

This may have been one of those moments in life where a simple choice could offer a radical change in life. Tom, for the first time, perhaps, was experiencing life in a place quite different to what he had known. Northallerton might have seemed a cut above Ryhope, Silksworth and the heavy industrial grind of Sunderland. A school like Bede might be a stepping stone to more education, perhaps even university, but his school reports were not signalling that potential. Nor was there money for that. So, more school might just defer entry to a rougher life than Northallerton seemed to offer. Even his temporary lodgings in Beaconsfield Road might have been better than home life in the Conservative Club in Hylton Road.

Tom's School Days

It is hard to avoid the thought that by now he had become aware of questions over his paternity. The very obvious albino features of Arnett and Eileen, impossible to hide: pale, translucent skin, and the effect on their eyesight: light would reach their retinas without passing through the control of the pupil, giving glare and their short sight – dark glasses were needed. That said, both seem to have enjoyed full lives, Eileen marrying twice. It would be well-known that this was an inherited characteristic and probably that the characteristic had to come from both parents.

So the arrival of dark-haired Amy might have been a relief to James Edgar and Hannah, that by the random ways of genes, the cards had shuffled differently. There was still a risk that a fourth child might revert to the albino outcome. This was still the era of large families: James Edgar had been one of five, with gaps between his siblings of 1, 3, 6 and 9 years, with long gaps often meaning the loss of a pregnancy, or perhaps more caution with the passage of time.

For James Edgar and Hannah their first child arrived 9 months after marriage, the next 4 years, then 5 years but Tom appeared only a little over 2 years after Amy in 1922. James Edgar and Hannah were still in their prime, under 40 years old, so this need not be unexpected. Equally, they might have agreed not to risk another child but despite an agreement, one appeared – James Edgar might have been surprised, after all they had… well, whatever.

Another issue might have been that as he grew up, Tom did not look or behave like his siblings. Families always have the "takes

Tom's School Days

after" conversations and bookish, studious, formal Tom might not have fitted, leaving questions. Arnett and Eileen were clearly a pair, Amy perhaps similar to them bar the albinism. Was there talk? Kids teasing?

Or perhaps the truth came out in some unexpected, ghastly way. The DNA testing gives a very strong clue who Tom's real father was. Did Hannah have a dalliance with Thomas Ferry, beyond one weekend in December 1921, and that became known? Did either Hannah or Thomas blurt it out – in the tight community of Silksworth it would be difficult to put that cat back in the bag?

Perhaps there was teasing, perhaps a rumour had gone round, perhaps James Edgar and Hannah had a row....Whether or not it was known, as Tom came to his last years of school, he had resolved to strike out on his own.

And did it matter? If one night of bliss remained a secret of then perhaps not. In those days families of four or more children were common.

James Edgar might not have known that the fourth child was not actually his. Or perhaps he was puzzled; perhaps he and Hannah were no longer close and so perhaps a further child was not expected.

Perhaps the liaison between Thomas Ferry and Hannah became known, perhaps it continued. At the time, the future for everyone was uncertain, Tom's origin may have been one of the family's lesser problems.

Tom's School Days

Hannah Isabel in 1932

One Awful Day. Perhaps?

Tom, just 16 years old, came home from school looking sheepish and furious. There was no one else in the house:

"Mam, there's been a row – Jimmy Ferry says that his dad Tommy is my dad too. That you had a dance with Tommy at Christmas, years ago, and things got heavy….."

"He says you went down the road with him – both a bit, you know…You nipped into Maggie's for a mess about and….

"He says his dad had a big row with his mum, Flo, and they weren't speaking for days; and that's why Flo doesn't speak to you".

"Well what would he know! I'm cross because the Ferrys didn't pay their bill..."

"Jimmy says you didn't want any more children on account of Arnett and Eileen being albino even though Amy turned out OK. So you pushed off Dad and you went with other men".

"I certainly did not! Never…, but Tommy Ferry did get friendly, very friendly, and I didn't expect owt to happen, and your dad was miserable about money…and Tommy bought me things… and your dad has been spending too much money at the Masonic Lodge, been good to himself with the car and that…".

One Awful Day. Perhaps?

"But you are my boy and I love you".

"I love you too, Mam".

There is no one left who knows if such a conversation took place or when.

Tom in yard in Silksworth: Sunday best, Sunday paper? (1932).

One Awful Day. Perhaps?

Maid, Arnett

Amy, Tom, Eileen

Grasping Nettles

But how it came about may not matter, if a golden opportunity emerged. Could the next few months reshape Tom's future radically?

His uncle, Wilfred George, was a manager at the Co-op in Ryhope. Uncle Frederick Ernest had a career as a telegraphist at the London and North Eastern Railway in Hull and his son, Tom's cousin, Clifford, was a clerk in Northallerton Council. Uncle Arthur Miles was Head Postmaster in Worthing, Sussex. These were Civil Service or similar appointments and it is likely that Tom saw something like that as his way forward. Once school life ended…

Already, even his sister Eileen had escaped to London, married to a police officer, and independent.

Hitler changed everything. Clearly, if the war progressed as might have been expected, some kind of military service was in prospect – once school was over. His cousin, Frank Miles, had been in the First World War from age 16 and was invalided out in 1918 with "constitutional tuberculosis". He was the only member of the family to have been in the forces. He died in 1940 having worked as a butcher.

Tom must have seen there was a risk of something similar. He might be conscripted to be a foot-soldier as he had no clear skills nor qualification. Continuing schooling, while waiting to be called, did not offer an attractive prospect. Even without a war, the end of school days could not lead to training or study: there was no money for that. Clifford and his uncles were in lives to be envied. Phyll said that Clifford was something of a hero in Tom's eyes. It is likely that during the early weeks in Northallerton, they chatted about how things were done and what possibilities existed.

The Government machine in London was moving rapidly and a key component was preparing local government for quite new roles. Tom, away from home in Northallerton, may have been alerted by Clifford to what was going on. In the Northallerton Council offices there would have been much work on preparing people and systems and Clifford would have been conscious of the local consequences. Already that had taken Bede School to Northallerton as Sunderland, with its mining, steel and ship building, was seen as a target. That had been achieved in just a few weeks. Clifford might have been aware of a relentless flow of information and instructions from Whitehall to all local authorities. Tom would have been excited by this and seen a huge opportunity which would be lost if he returned to Ryhope. He needed to plan and act.

In April 1939 legislation had been passed to provide that males aged 20 and 21 years old could be called up for six months full-time military training. This came into force in June but was superseded by the National Service (Armed Forces) Act on 3 September 1939, which enforced full conscription on all male British subjects between 18 and 41. Tom reached age 17 on

Grasping Nettles

8 September and so might have continued at school for another year. Then another door opened.

In September 1939, the traditional method of entry to the Home Civil Service, by examination, was suspended and recruitment to clerical vacancies in Government Departments, changed.

> "Those who cannot be supplied by the loan of staff from other Departments were filled on a temporary basis through the employment department of the Ministry of Labour and National Service".

The Civil Service examinations would normally have been held in September but now this was an opportunity – perhaps through the Labour Exchange in Northallerton. Tom might have known other lads keen to move on in their lives in this way. Real fighting in the war did not start until May 1940, as the Allies' strategy was to allow time for economic and naval superiority to build up military resources.

We can guess that Tom, perhaps guided by Clifford, applied through the Labour Exchange to join the Civil Service. He would have come over as a bright, lively, aware young man. He would interview well, he had good handwriting, and was methodical. This, in war-time, would be an adequate substitute for a solid Civil Service examination. The preparations for war had been in hand for some time. Maybe, Clifford was able to smooth the path, applying "more flies caught by treacle…".

The London Gazette, the daily journal of record for the British Government and its agencies, included in its edition of 22

Grasping Nettles

December 1939 a long list assignments of civil servants. Included in the Clerical Class was "Thomas Wilfred Pearson" who was assigned to the Air Ministry with a "Certificate of Qualification" issued on 25th September. It sounds rather grand but all Civil Service appointments were announced in this way. Other news in that 74 page edition was a "Proclamation by the King Appointing the First Day of January 1940 as a Bank Holiday throughout England, Wales and Northern Ireland".

So Tom's education ended, and he was off to London, starting in the Air Ministry on 6 December 1939.

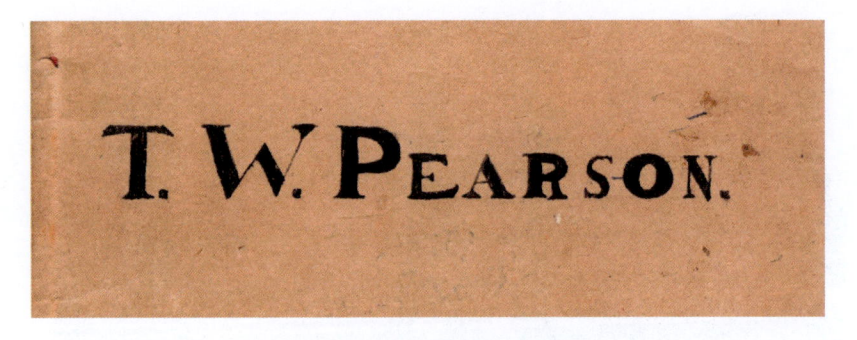

Tom's report book cover

Grasping Nettles

A New Life Altogether

London was famous for smog, a poisonous combination of thick smoke from coal fires and a cold fog rising from the River Thames. This was quite different to the Haar of the east coast. Even so Claude Monet visited London three times to paint scenes of fog: he claimed: "Without fog London would not be beautiful." Romantic when viewed through these eyes but deadly, and smog was not brought under control until the late 1950s. For Tom, suddenly, everything changed. London was vast, almost incomprehensible, compared to Sunderland, masses of people, smart people, cars, bustle, money, huge buildings, cinema, theatre, this was one of the great cities of the world and he was part of it. Almost nothing in his life up until then had or even could have prepared him for this. And he was to be part of the Government effort to aircraft to deal with the enemy – he was part of the war effort. He must have been thrilled and terrified.

Tom's sister, Eileen May Pearson, was born in October 1915, and by the outbreak of war she was married to Samuel Clarke and living in 24 Gloucester Close, Willesden, London. At the time of their marriage on 27 July 1938, Sam was a turner but there was ambition around – he wanted to be a police officer. His son, Peter Lawrence Clarke, suggested, during that afternoon we had in the sun in 2003, that Sam was too short to meet the entry requirements of the Durham Constabulary but

A New Life Altogether

that the Metropolitan Police, in London, was less demanding. This provided an escape route from the suffocating narrow streets of Sunderland. Sam became PC 237C in London on 15 August 1938 and the couple moved into Gloucester Close, which may have been police housing. Today it is quite smart 4 storey blocks of flats, which might date from that time. Their son, Peter, was born on 7 June 1939. By early 1940, it is easy to think that Tom was lodging with the Clarkes and commuting into Whitehall.

He was initially assigned to the Air Ministry but in May 1940 the Ministry of Aircraft Production was formed by the Prime Minister, Winston Churchill, to produce large numbers of aircraft to fight the Battle of Britain. The first minister was Lord Beaverbrook, who had built the Daily Express into the most successful mass-circulation newspaper in the world. Under his control the Ministry presided over an enormous increase in British aircraft production.

> "Personnel were recruited from outside the Air Ministry, interaction was informal, characterised by personal intervention, crisis management and application of willpower to improve output. Few records were kept, the functions of most individuals were left undefined and business was conducted mainly over the telephone."

It must be this way of working that appealed to Tom and he thrived on it – his "can do" attitude developed and stayed with him.

A New Life Altogether

Now, Tom would be going to work in a jacket and tie, white shirt, polished shoes, entering grand offices which radiated power and importance. He was working in Shell-Mex House, a vast Art Deco office on the Thames Embankment, in which the new Ministry of Aircraft Production (MAP) was created in May 1940. There he met Phyllis Connie Dawkins, also working in MAP, a year older than him and very confident about London.

Shell-Mex House

The end of the 19th century brought to a close the country way of life that the Pearsons in northern England, and Phyll's family, the Dawkins and Bennetts, in Essex and Oxfordshire, had led for centuries in different ways. There are probably half a dozen unrelated Dawkins tribes, with little in common apart from the name,

A New Life Altogether

Phyll's had been blacksmiths and farmers in Stapleford Tawney, near Romford in Essex. There were many generations in this family, all centred around horses and the forge. At the end of the 19th century, they had taken their horse knowledge into London, driving cabs and joining the Army in the Royal Field Artillery. They had been Farrier Sergeants in the Royal Field Artillery, leading teams of horse pulling gun carriages – in India, the South African or Boer War of 1898-1901 and then in France and India in the First World War. The gun carriages were drawn by 6 horses with three riders – still seen on ceremonial occasions in the Royal Parks. After the war, much of the family congregated in Willesden, in north London.

Leonard Godfrey Dawkins was Phyll's father.

The Bennetts came from Clifton Hampden and nearby villages in Berkshire and Oxford, lived the classic rural English village life, with many children and, presumably what would now be seen as poverty. It may be the life seen in Stella Gibbon's "Cold Comfort Farm" (published in 1932) and subject to similar massive disruption as the modern 20th century arrived.

Phyll's mother was Hilda Jubilee Bennett, born to Rachel Champ in 1897 which was Queen Victoria's Jubilee year. Hilda was the 13th of 14 children (although the last might actually have been her niece – that happened). Her eldest brother, William Jesse Bennett, was 24 years older than her and so she had a niece a year older than her. In the Bennett tribe they had several sons called Jesse. Having sired 14 offspring, Hilda's father Jesse Bennett died in 1901, aged 51, in Benson (then

A New Life Altogether

called Bensington). By this time some of the Bennett family had given up the land and moved to London. Others went to Wales, Australia and New Zealand. Rachel went too and by 1911 was a cloakroom attendant in Marylebone. The same year Hilda left school and started work in a chemist's shop. She spent the First World War in the workshop of Waring and Gillow (normally furniture makers) packing cannon shells with gunpowder.

In 1919 Hilda married Leonard Godfrey Dawkins who, by then, had given up horses and cabs and was working as a fishmonger, in Sainsburys and later Gow's in Old Broad Street and in due course they moved into Carpenter Street Flats in Mayfair.

A New Life Altogether

The last few years of Hilda's working life was as a book-keeper at Garrard & Co, then the Crown Jewellers based in Albemarle Street, a short walk from Carpenter Street. She collected various items, put in to Garrard for repair but mostly irreparable, including a pewter teapot which had been caught in a gas flame, melting a hole that could not be repaired, as pewter melts at very low temperatures. In contrast, during the War she was paid by Garrard with some solid silver soup spoons, in lieu of pay.

Phyll was living at home with her parents, in Carpenter Street just behind Berkeley Square, in the very heart of Mayfair. She was much taken by the glamour of her neighbours, even though her family was quite poor. To Phyll, the excitement of living and working in the very heart of the world, as Britain saw itself, stayed with her for the rest of her life. The cinema was at its height, dancing was popular and a social life was available. The early months of the War seemed exciting and romantic.

In just a few months, Tom grew from being a schoolboy to something closer to a 'man about town' during the 'phoney war', which had ended on 10 May 1940 with the appointment of Churchill as Prime Minister.

Phyll was working in the MAP division which recruited cabinet-makers to build the airframes of the first of the de Havilland Mosquitos which appeared early in 1941, initially for reconnaissance and then as a light bomber. It had a wooden structure and, at first, avoided the weight of any armament, so that with twin Merlin engines it was faster than contemporary fighters. In time it became one of the most famous RAF types

A New Life Altogether

developed during the war. Britain had been well served by experts in the uses of timber, from merchants to carpenters, joiners and cabinet makers, and they had been largely recruited into firms making trainer aircraft. The parent firm, de Havilland, was one of those, and then became the lead contractor for a group producing the Mosquito. Manufacture of components up to fuselages, wings and empennages (the tail structure of a plane) was dispersed to firms formerly in the furniture industry. The total of all marques of Mosquito produced in Britain during the war was nearly 7,000, and it was also built in Canada and Australia.

In 2006, the BBC collected war-time memories from ordinary people. One from Margaret Collinge recorded that after school she did the Civil Servants' exam for Clerical Officers (the one that Tom bypassed as it had been suspended) and was offered a job in London, which at first she refused.

> *At the age of 19 I decided to accept the job. I was very nervous, but had a friend who had also gone to work in London. I lived at various girls' hostels, including the Girl Guide Hostel in Palace Street, until I was 'thrown out' at the age of 21. I then moved to one in Vincent Square which got bombed ~ the flats behind it were hit by a Doodlebug. It was a Sunday morning and I saw it coming as I was walking onto the stair head. There was glass flying around and I got a cut on my arm. This was the same day as they bombed the Guards' Chapel and a lot of the guards were killed ~ it was the worst I*

A New Life Altogether

remember. After that four of us went to live in a flat in Hampstead.

I had worked for the Air Ministry for two years before the War started and this expanded during the War to include the Ministry of Aircraft Production and then later, the Ministry of ~ all in the same office. I did finance work and I had to work on the costs for things for works and buildings related to aircraft factories. I was authorised to spend up to £2,000, which was a lot at the time. I would telephone the factories but would also meet people from them to discuss things.

I used the tube and buses to get to work. You got used to the danger and if the air raid siren went you got yourself into the nearest substantial building. Sometimes I carried a gas mask. I had my lunch at the Ministry and cooked for myself at other times.

In 1941 the Ministry was evacuated to Harrogate for two years. The offices were divided amongst various big hotels and I worked in the Crown Hotel and was billeted with a very nice lady. Back in London we put the radio on at lunchtime on VE Day and heard the news about the end of the War in Europe. There were masses of people in all the squares and I joined them in the afternoon, but it all got a 'bit too much' for me! There were similar celebrations on VJ Day.

A New Life Altogether

Phyll and Tom were certainly evacuated like that to Harrogate. Other memories recorded like this mention Starbeck, a village on the edge of Harrogate, which is where Phyll and Tom were also billeted, so there was quite an "ex-pat" community. This was Phyll's first time living away from home, free from the control of a rather stern father who was, perhaps, overfond of a drink. The town was elegant, it was a resort, so the hotels were large and well-appointed.

Even if romance had not started between the filing cabinets of Shell-Mex House, Harrogate provided golden opportunities for Phyll and Tom equally to start new lives – probably together. "Betty's Tearooms" definitely were burned into Phyll's memories.

Tom worked at MAP for almost 2 years, acquiring administrative skills, using his education, intelligence and losing his Sunderland accent. Inevitably, he was called up for military service and enlisted with the Royal Army Service Corps (RASC) on 4 December 1941, aged 19 years and 3 months; beginning at the 60th (Welsh) Holding Unit in Cardiff. The RASC was responsible for land, coastal and lake transport; air despatch; supply of food, water, fuel, and general domestic stores such as clothing, and stationery(but not ammunition and military and technical equipment, which were the responsibility of the Royal Army Ordnance Corps); administration of barracks; the Army Fire Service; and provision of staff clerks to headquarters units.

A New Life Altogether

The assignment to the RASC clearly recognised his previous two years employment in the Ministry of Aircraft Production. He "ceased to be attached" to the Holding Unit and was posted to No 12 Royal Army Service Corps Training Branch where he was given 8 days leave ending on 23 January 1942, which was Phyll's birthday. They were already close.

He was "mustered" as a Clerk IIIA on 22 January 1942, then reclassified as Clerk IIIB on 21 May 1942, and again to Clerk II on 1 September 1942. There were courses and tests to be passed on each advancement – Tom's war so far had been far from the fighting.

Meanwhile the war had spread round the planet. By this time France had been making treaties (Armistices) with the Italians and the Germans; but France was breaking in two.

Operation "Torch" was the outcome of an agreement between the British and United States governments to invade French North Africa. It was agreed in the summer of 1942 with the objective of seizing the German and Italian airfields in Tunisia, and hoping that the enemy could be driven out of Africa, freeing up the Mediterranean sea routes, in preparation for an invasion of Sicily and Italy. This was a vast operation to provide all the equipment and personnel to be able to take over the south coast of the Mediterranean, thus opening a second front against Germany. It was the first mass involvement of US troops in Europe and saw the first large-scale airborne assault carried out by the United States.

A New Life Altogether

There were three separate forces: the western landing at Casablanca, the central at Oran and the eastern, the British, at Algiers. The role of the British forces was to aim immediately for Tunis, 500 miles away. The British force would have 200,000 men and 35,000 vehicles. Landing began on 8 November.

Tom was posted to North Africa as a Private on 22 December 1942, (a year after being called up) arriving at HQ in Algiers on 14 March 1943. The gap suggests that there was a preparatory period in Britain and then a troopship to North Africa. He was made a Corporal 3 weeks later from 5 April 1943. We know little or nothing of his time there. He jokingly said was that he "chased Rommel across the desert armed with his typewriter" and that he lost his typewriter in a crossing between ships, but presumably another was procured.

Algeria was ruled as a colony from 1830 to 1848, and then as a *département*, an integral part of France, from November 1848. In the 1940s there must have been political concerns in Britain invading such French sovereign territory, when the original Arab population had been subjugated for over a century. The instability in the country continued for decades after the war.

There is a huge volume (700 pages) "The Story of the RASC 1939-45" which describes in detail the North African operations and its work in other theatres of war. The invasion involved over 360,000 personnel for which supplies had to be brought in by fleets of ships, stored and moved forward to the front. In effect a major city was imported in just a few days. Being part

A New Life Altogether

of the organisation of this would have exactly suited Tom. The quantities were huge but at some points the Allies attack forces were moving forward faster than their supplies could manage. The action began on 24 November, was complete by mid-May 1943 and the "Axis" forces removed from Africa, as they retreated into Europe. Tom is listed in the "Roll of Honour" in the Story.

It looks as though he was based in Algiers and I have a book he owned, written in French. This was "L'Algérie" by Clement Alzonne – Tom signed it on the fly sheet adding "Algiers Nov 1942". The dates do not line up, but the RASC history talks about many ships being held off the coast in November and December. He acquired must have acquired that very soon after arriving in November – perhaps he was not held back on the ships but was able to enter Algiers ahead of the main force. He

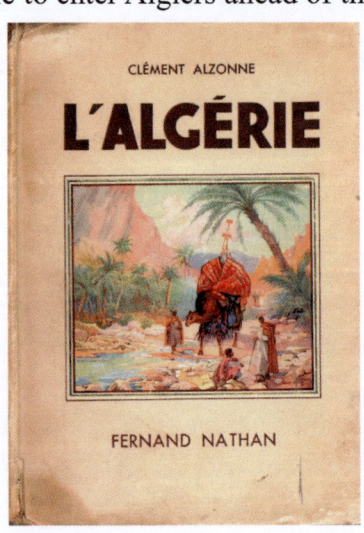

A New Life Altogether

could then have found the book abandoned by rapidly departing Italian officials as the Allies team took over offices.

The next page is stamped "Commissione Italiana Armistizio Con La Francia" (the Commission for the Italian Armistice with France) and "Delegazione Navale per l'Africa Settentrionale" (Naval Delegation for North Africa). The book is a classic, illustrated, history of Algeria in French which he clearly could read. At the end of the war he was declared to have a good command of French – then the language of diplomacy and of Algeria.

His mother, Hannah Isabella, died on 9 September 1943 – his Army record shows he changed his next of kin to his father, James Edgar Pearson, that day. It is odd that he had originally given his mother as next of kin – it is probable that she had been ill for some time, perhaps several years. It is another hint that family life in Sunderland was probably uncomfortable – had his parents been at loggerheads? His father was almost 60 years old and would not have been called for military service – had Hannah cooperated in helping Tom leave home, even with the obvious dangers of a military role?

Four days later, on 13 September, he was promoted to (Acting) Sergeant. Acting Warrant Sergeant followed on 11 December 1944. before being promoted to Staff Sergeant and assigned to the Central Military Force in Italy in May 1945. The European war was over, leaving vast areas devastated and much reconstruction needed: not just the infrastructure but whole systems for running a country.

A New Life Altogether

What was he doing? Certainly little or nothing with a weapon. The Army gave him scope to develop his administrative and management skills – the large deployment of men brought huge demands for food and catering, vehicles and fuel in a country that had probably been a sleepy backwater of the French empire. Virtually everything would have to be assessed, ordered and deployed. As a Sergeant he would be responsible for a unit, have men to command and to answer for. He might well have been using his French (quickly advanced from his Bede School instruction) in engaging with the local services and authorities. He ended the war less than 23 years old but with far more experience than Sunderland could have ever offered.

A New Life Altogether

Staff Sergeant Thomas Wilfred Pearson

Life in London

The war with Germany ended on 7 May 1945 and Japan surrendered on 2 September after the use of the first atomic bombs on Hiroshima and Nagasaki. Tom returned to London on 19 August 1945.

The wedding was at the Dawkins' local church, St George's, Hanover Square, which as the Parish Church of Mayfair also happened to be the "go to" place for grand society weddings. President Teddy Roosevelt, Guglielmo Marconi and endless members of the aristocracy had been married there (as well as "Eliza Doolittle's" father Alfred, who was "getting married in the morning"). The service was conducted by the Hon. Venerable Stephen Henry Phillimore, Archdeacon of Middlesex. Tom became a sidesman at the church later.

Phyll organised the whole show; she had no option as Tom was in Algiers, with no telephone and only terse military telegrams possible. So she set up the wedding she wanted, planned to the last detail, at short notice. It was to be on Tom's birthday, 8 September, when he would be 23 years old, just 6 years after leaving school and his family in September 1939. He was granted 28 days leave until 27 September.

Phyll would have been used to society weddings in her local church; so she would have known what it should be like. But she was living at home, in a flat rented from the Church

Life in London

Commissioners, sharing "facilities" with the neighbours. They didn't even have their own loo. She had a good job in the Civil Service and so should Tom on return from war. There would be only one wedding and it was to be a great one; for which she probably had been saving up.

On 23 August, the Portman Press Bureau, Sloane Street, accepted Phyll's booking to take "photographs outside St George's, Hanover Square for which rough proofs would be taken to the reception for approval before sending to the "Tatler" "Queen" etc". Proofs were indeed provided: three 8" by 6" prints for £5 6s and 6d – which probably included the photographer's fee.

On 29 August, Phyll bought a "solid gold wedding ring" from Bravingtons Ltd, 6 Grand Buildings, Strand, Trafalgar Square for £1 and 5 shillings. The next day, 30 August, a letter came from Mrs W. Thompson who provided "Board Residence and Bed and Breakfast" at "Grimscar", 112 Trafalgar Road, near Peasholm, Scarborough. Mrs Thompson wrote that she had a letter from her son Frank, asking to reserve "a bedroom, with full board, for your wife and self from 9 September for fourteen days". I guess that Tom knew Frank. The price was 10 shillings each per day. However, "it was necessary to bring emergency cards and ration books for points, also own towels as we are not allowed coupons for these".

On 1 September, Phyll wrote to the Great Northern Hotel, Kings Cross, London, the railway hotel, to book a double room for 8 September – the Manager acknowledged the booking on

Life in London

Tuesday 4 September. The bill was paid on 9 September: £1 and 11 pence,

A "second-hand 9 carat Ladies Signet Ring" was bought on 7 September from Robertsons, Diamond Merchants at 199-201 Edgware Road. I have the ring, which was engraved "TWP" and is well-worn. My fingers are too large to put it on – I guess Tom's thin young fingers needed a Ladies size. At double the price of wedding ring, it must have been the engraving that pushed up the price.

Flowers were ordered from "Fresh Flowers Ltd" 47 Davies Street, W1 (and paid for on the wedding day):

>Bouquet £2 5s
>Posies £1 1s (a guinea)
>Spray 5s 6d
>2 Buttonholes £3

The wedding took place at 2pm at St George's, Hanover Square, followed by a reception at St George's Institute, Broadbent St, W.1 – which was associated with the church and had been provided by the Duke of Westminster. The photographs show a "radiant" bride (a cliché but true) and a thin, nervous-looking groom. Both families were properly represented.

Phyll's wedding present to him was a Conway Stewart "Duro" fountain pen in "cracked black ice" with a 14k gold nib, reflecting his profession and something he could keep close to

Life in London

him. The thick nib left a characteristic mark on any document he touched thereafter.

Phyll must have been ecstatic and Tom stunned. He had been making a career in army organisation, in Algiers and soon in Naples, and his new wife had pulled together a perfect event. Her sister Eileen was the bridesmaid and Tom's nephew, Peter Clarke was there too, age 6, in a velvet-collared coat, with his mother, Eileen, and Amy, both Tom's sisters. I have two dried buttonholes, and remnants of the bouquet containing myrtle – used for Royal wedding bouquets since that of Queen Victoria, and Phyll as a devoted Royalist would have known that.

Life in London

The reception must have been lively. Phyll's colleagues produced a card with over 40 signatures and there were telegrams, from James Edgar (signed "Dad"), Arnett and Biddy (who had married in 1943), Jimmy Gibson (who would marry Amy in November that year) Harriet and Eva (her daughter) then more from Brighton, Stoke Newington, Cheltenham, Bognor Regis, and one addressed to Sergeant and Mrs Pearson. A Cable and Wireless "wire" arrived from Don, Phyll's brother, who was on a naval boat somewhere either in the Far East or on the Arctic Convoys.

The wedding night was spent at the Great Northern Hotel and the next day the train took them to Scarborough – 250 miles, and only 54 miles from Sunderland. Tom probably had been to Scarborough before.

It was lively with live shows and cinema. The couple went to:

> Dancing at the Spa Ballroom at 8.30pm on 13 September and another night.
>
> *Hedley Claxton's "Frivolities of 1945"* at Caitlin's Arcadia on Foreshore Road on Saturday 15 September
>
> *A Grand Gala* with The Spa Orchestra and The Spa Singers on Sunday 16 September
>
> *The Bouquets* at the Spa Theatre on Wednesday 19 September
>
> There was also a visit to the North Bay Bathing Pool (Tom was a keen swimmer)

Life in London

Life in London

They left Mrs Thompson's hospitality on 21 September – 3 days earlier than booked.

Did they make a trip to Sunderland in those next few days? Today making that trip by train involves several changes so a day trip is unlikely but then things may have been different. It is hard to see when that first visit was otherwise made; Tom's army record does not contain any obvious home leave. By 27 September they were back in London spending the evening at the Palladium Theatre. The next day, Tom left for Naples.

The war was over, the world was covered in debris and destroyed communities.

Even with the enemy defeated there was much to do in clearing up and rebuilding Europe. The structures of government across Europe had been obliterated requiring a continued military-type capacity and presence. Tom embarked for Milan on 2 October 1945 to be part of the Central Military Force which was rebuilding the governance and systems of a population in shock and poverty. There he was Chief Clerk to "Q" Branch which handled logistics, supply, transport, clothing, and maintenance.

He was a changed man. At Christmas he sent a 78rpm gramophone record, lasting 1 minute, made by "Voices of the Forces". He recorded a personal message to Phyll, Hilda, Len and Eileen too. He hoped to be home soon. But his voice! There is no trace of his Sunderland accent, he sounds like a senior officer, and so formal, even with his wife. Perhaps he was

Life in London

conscious of, perhaps embarrassed by, the engineer making the recording. Even so, he was now someone quite different.

There was fun too: the Army established the Naples Area Turf Club which held race meetings at "Sandown Park Race Course, Casoria" part of an extensive array of opportunities. In the race meetings of 1946, on 17 March and 28 April, Staff Sergeant Pearson is shown as the "owner" of horses "San Fairy Ann" and "Another Christian". The programme for 28 April "informs that the Turf Club is winding up with a final "bumper" meeting on 12 May 1946".

A constitutional referendum was held on 2 June, a day celebrated since as "Festa della Repubblica", the Italian monarchy was abolished, having been associated with the deprivations of the war and the Fascist rule, and Italy became a republic.

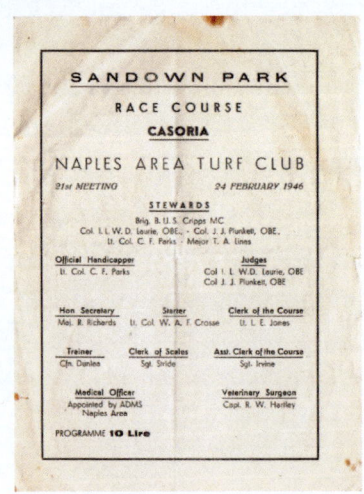

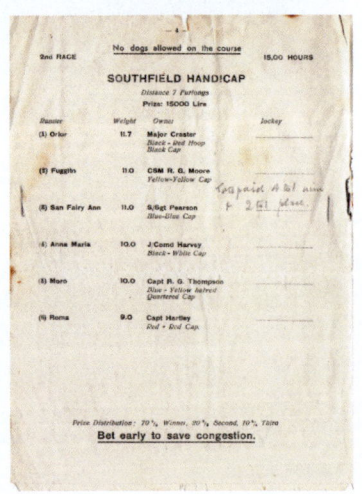

Life in London

Home

Tom returned to Britain.

Phyll was setting up home in Mayfair, probably soon after the wedding. At 24 years old she was free; she may have given up work as Tom was likely to return from the war to a good job and a fair salary and married women were not expected (perhaps not permitted) to work. Rationing was introduced during the war to manage the limited outputs of goods and this continued until the ending of meat rationing in July 1945.

Phyll's work during the war was on recruiting cabinet makers to build the Mosquito bomber – a wooden plane. Fuselages, wings and tailplanes were made at furniture companies such as Ronson, E. Gomme ("G Plan"), Parker Knoll, Parslow Furniture, Austinsuite and Styles & Mealing. Wing spars were made by J. B. Heath and Dancer & Hearne. Now she went to Heals in Tottenham Court Road to buy furniture from these same companies – she had ration coupons to permit a dining table and four chairs; and she bought quite a lot of other things for the flat. She was proud that on completion of the deal, the salesman suggested that as she had bought so much she could have a square of carpet as well.

On 9 July 1946 Tom returned to Britain and was discharged from the Army on 16 November 1946. Two days later, 18 November 1946, he and Phyll moved to 8 Bourdon Flats,

Home

Bourdon Street, London W1. This was right in the very heart of London, only minutes from Selfridges, Marble Arch and Berkeley Square. At that time, such homes were not expensive to rent – today a one bedroom flat in that street can easily cost £2 million to buy.

Tom was transferred to the Army Reserve, Royal Army Service Corps, on 23 November 1946; he had returned to the Ministry of Supply and became a Higher Executive Officer in the Establishments and Organisation Division.

In July 1949, I was born at St George's Hospital, Marble Arch, a building which is now the 5 star Lanesborough Hotel, just a few minutes walk from home in Bourdon Street.

In October 1950, Tom was seconded to the Iron and Steel Corporation of Great Britain, so once again he was based in Shell-Mex House, which lies between The Embankment and the Strand.

Following the 1945 election of Attlee's Labour government, the Iron and Steel Act 1949, which received the Royal Assent on 24 November, brought 94 iron and steel companies into public ownership and vested them in the Iron and Steel Corporation of Great Britain, which took office in October 1950. Vesting date was 15 February 1951. Unlike the nationalisation of the coal industry, where assets rather than undertakings were transferred to public ownership, this left intact the organisation of the individual companies which continued to operate under boards appointed by the Corporation. Tom took "the greater part of the

Home

pioneer work in staffing, accommodation and kindred matters" in setting up the Corporation as recorded in a letter of appreciation of 15 January 1951 from S.S. Wilson on behalf of the Board, enclosing a cheque for £40.

No fundamental structural changes had been achieved by the autumn of 1951 when the Conservative Party returned to office, pledged to denationalise the industry. This was brought about by the Iron and Steel Act 1953.

Phyll would have a full time job looking after her new baby, setting up her new home. Her brother Don, 5 years younger, had returned home after hostilities in the Far East ended where he had been a ships telegraphist in the Royal Navy. He had lied about his age and concealed his colour blindness to sign up but had probably not bargained for his ship becoming part of the Arctic convoys supplying places like Murmansk. For this in he was awarded the Russian Federation Ushakov Medal for Arctic Convoys Veterans. Don married Audrey Marshall in March 1950 and they lived not far away so there was emerging a lively young scene in central London; but not for long.

The Banks of the Clyde

Tom's secondment to the Iron and Steel Corporation ended and he, Phyll and I moved to Glasgow in 1951. Tom was, probably, being tried out by being given a wider role. It was normal to give capable young civil servants regular changes to expand their experience. He was to manage the finance section of the Royal Ordnance Factory in Beardmore Street, Dalmuir on Clydebank which was converted in 1951 to manufacture armoured fighting vehicles. The factory is now the site of the Golden Jubilee Hospital and associated Beardmore Hotel. The terms of such secondment usually included providing help with accommodation. So they were able to make a home in a smart bungalow at 18 Berwick Drive, Cardonald, which must have been quite a shock to Phyll, who had always lived in down-at-heel flats in or around Mayfair, albeit in the smartest parts of London. They recorded the move on Tom's National Registration Identity Card from 18 September 1951.

It was not so strange to Tom, who had been assigned to Pollok for some months for initial training in the war. He was used to people with strong accents, as the Sunderland and North Yorkshire voices were far from the "received pronunciation" of London. He was used to people who worked in mines, worked with their hands, and worked hard. Even so, he had also taken on a life in Whitehall, with grand titles and even grander offices. In London, Selfridges had been round the corner, the local shop

The Banks of the Clyde

was in Berkeley Square and the streets were thronged with smart people. He was between two worlds.

In Cardonald, there was a garden front and back with several steps up to the front and back doors. It was on a corner with Fife Avenue which sloped down to Paisley Road West. Each day Tom would set off on foot to travel by tram, crossing the Clyde on the Renfrew ferry.

He was leaving Phyll and me in a strange, cold place. I (from the age of 4) made a friend in fellow toddler Jacky and learned to imitate the sound of the bagpipes by holding my nose, humming the tune and giving vibrato by banging my throat. I also learned to speak with two accents, Scottish outside home and Tom and Phyll's increasingly neutral English. Phyll made some trips to the bustling shopping centre of Glasgow – but it wasn't London.

London had been through bad winters; in 1947, snow and fog brought Britain to a halt for 55 days. The River Thames froze for the first time in 200 years and people skated on it. There were many power cuts – and food and heating were in short supply. It is likely that Phyll was concerned that 1952 would be much the same. It was the year of the Great Smog; frost and fog strangled shipping movements at the start of December 1952. On Monday 1 December of that year, the Greenock Telegraph revealed the Clyde was "still closed to shipping movements due to the lack of visibility. No large vessels had stirred on the river since Friday of the previous week".

The Banks of the Clyde

Phyll had always been reserved and shy which could be seen as "snobbish" – the more so in Glasgow where the normal accent would have seemed strident, at the very least, to her. Their changed circumstances – going from Carpenter Street, sharing a bath and lavatory with two other families, to their own flat in Bourdon Street and now a detached bungalow with a garden, might have helped, but possibly did not. Looking back at that period, it seems probable that Phyll suffered from post-natal depression and, possibly, agoraphobia (which seems to recur in the family). Whatever the cause, the young love idyll was beginning to fade for her. She adored Tom but she missed much of her previous life.

Meanwhile Tom was in his organising element – already evident from his months as part of the team setting up the Iron and Steel Corporation. Soon after starting his new post in "S.C. Accounts", in charge of a good many clerical officers, he began to notice oddnesses in the way the work was organised. It seemed that people who had to work together did not sit at adjacent desks as might be expected nor passed files to one another, instead they waited for a messenger to collect and deliver, even just across the room. Eventually, he asked the obvious question "what is the rationale for these arrangements?" He might have expressed it in a softer way in case there was some blindingly obvious reason for the long-standing arrangement. But there wasn't.

The answer was simple but impossible for him to have guessed. It was just that the Roman Catholics sat together and the Protestants likewise. Tom had a strong religious core; he had

The Banks of the Clyde

named his son after the Archdeacon of Middlesex, but this was a set-up he could not tolerate. People were asked and persuaded to move desks, efficiency was recognised to have improved and a small step in community cohesion had been achieved.

Other aspects of Scottish life emerged. Not only did civil servants work on Saturday mornings (sports jackets and flannels permitted rather than three-piece suits) but Christmas Day was not a public holiday. The Scots had their own bank notes, issued by the three main Scottish banks. Pubs closed at 10pm. Tom delighted in the New Year rituals of laying a fresh fire for lighting after midnight and first footing, with coal, bread, salt and a dram.

The King died on 6 February 1952. He and the Queen had been at the heart of British war-time defiance. Phyll had lived all her life within walking distance of Buckingham Palace. The Princesses Elizabeth and Margaret lived in areas to which she and her sister, Eileen, could relate. Phyll had followed the saga of Edward VIII and Mrs Simpson in horror and now poor George VI was gone – without Phyll being able to make daily direct contact with London life.

The BBC 405-line black and white television service in Scotland started from Kirk o' Shotts on 14 March 1952 using low power reserve transmitters and broadcast the King's funeral procession, live from the heart of London. It closed down for completion of the installation and full service began on 17 August 1952.

The Banks of the Clyde

My first childhood recollection was being woken late in the evening of 22 January 1953 and brought into my parents' bedroom. My sister had been born, only minutes before, at home – and was to be christened Janet Claire. Actually, the original intention was that she should be Valerie Ann but Phyll was uncertain about the Scots' pronunciation of that so registration of the birth was delayed and Janet Claire recorded only just within the legal time limit. So late was this that the silver christening mug presented by Phyll's sister, Eileen, had to be amended by a silver shield over the original initials.

The Coronation of Queen Elizabeth II was televised on 2 June 1953 and watched by the Pearson family and many friends and neighbours on the new television set bought by Tom. The cost of the television set was around £100: Tom's salary in 1949 was £675 p.a, so this purchase was huge for a family with very young children. Tom probably thought this would help lessen Phyll's homesickness for the life of London, made worse by postnatal depression.

Even with this vast investment, on 20 August 1953 Tom requested a transfer from the Royal Ordnance Factory. He was well thought of in the Ministry of Supply and the transfer was supported on compassionate grounds but by 15 October no reply had been given. This was because preparations were being made in the Ministry to fill five vacancies for Senior Executive Officers. He was to be told that his "request for transfer is still under consideration and will be treated sympathetically".

The Banks of the Clyde

"If granted his transfer will still be within the Royal Ordnance Factory organisation as our shortages at H.E.O level are too serious to permit of the loss of someone with Mr Pearson's experience".

Hilda and Len

Let's go back to the Dawkins for a moment. They were the only family we knew and their origins have much in common with the Pearsons and many others. In some ways Phyll and Tom ploughed their own furrows, not drawing on family resources (of mind nor of money); they made a fresh start.

"Nana has broken the back axle!" Tom realised that to make light of the failure of this, his first car, a green Ford Popular 100E, registration MOR 20, he needed to blame, albeit affectionately, his mother-in-law Hilda. His two children, Jan and I, were in the car and something serious had happened. Hilda was visiting the family in our new house in Basingstoke. Hilda liked her son-in-law who was funny, intelligent and warm.

Hilda Jubilee Bennett was born on 14 May 1897 and named to recognise Queen Victoria's Diamond Jubilee to be celebrated in June that year. She was the second youngest of 14 children to Jesse Bennett, a repairer of agricultural machinery and a taxidermist, and Rachel Champ. Hilda suggested that her younger sister, Dora, was in fact her niece, conceived in irregular circumstances and added to the stable. Her eldest brother, William Jesse Bennett, was born in 1873 and by the time of Hilda's birth he was working as a baker in Oxford; several of the Bennett boys worked in bread and cake making. The family was brought up in Benson (formerly Bensington)

Hilda and Len

near Long Wittenham, the village from which Rachel Champ came. Two miles away was Clifton Hampden, the home of the Bennett family, who had been farm workers for generations.

Hilda and Len

Cowley and Oxford were not far away and there was a family story that a member of the family had been a partner of William Morris in his cycle business in James Street, Cowley. This Bennett certainly lived in James Street but not at the same time as Lord Nuffield – an aspirational myth amongst many in the family. As agriculture mechanised, labouring on farming declined and the Bennett offspring drifted into London for work, finally abandoning Benson when Jesse died from a stroke in April 1901 in 1 Brook Street, aged 51. Rachel, still with young children at home, moved to Marylebone and in 1911 was working as a cloakroom attendant. She died in 1934, aged 81.

Hilda lived with Rachel in 39 Marylebone Lane, St Marylebone, and attended St Thomas' School, Orchard Street leaving there in 1911 to work in Squire's Chemists, Oxford Street. The following year she is in Morny, a perfumer of 201 Regent Street, as a packer. During the First World War she worked in Waring & Gillows, Regent Street, filling shells with gunpowder.

Across London, Leonard Godfrey Dawkins was the eldest child in his family – he was born on 7 July 1895 in Camberwell as his family also made the transition from rural to city. The Dawkins family had been based in Stapleford Tawney or nearby Stapleford Abbotts, in Essex, since at least 1763 – as blacksmiths and wheelwrights, work based around agriculture and horses. In 1871, his grandfather, Samuel Dawkins, had been a Census Enumerator, a prosperous, respected figure who left a bold signature in the Enumerator's Book.

Hilda and Len

There were three families in and around Little Heath in Essex who were close: the Dawkins, the Spurges and the Shackladys. In 1865 Samuel married Emily Shacklady whose family farmed at Little Heath. Their first child, born in 1867, William Shacklady Dawkins, later set up as a blacksmith in Brighton at 110 London Road. Emily died in March 1872, giving birth to her stillborn fourth child. A substantial memorial to Emily was placed in a Chadwell church, later demolished. Samuel then in July 1873 married her sister, Georgiana, an act illegal at the time, presumably to look after his three sons and they had a further five children of which three survived. They knew the marriage was illegal; it took place in St James' Westminster rather than the more obvious Great Ilford church used for Samuel's first marriage. His will left everything to Georgiana, described as his sister-in-law, not his wife.

The links between the three families are made clear by the names of the children of Emily and Georgiana's brother John who married Sarah Spurge. These include John Spurge Shacklady and Samuel Dawkins Shacklady.

Samuel Dawkins' two other sons, Ernest Samuel and Leonard George both went into the Army as farrier sergeants in the Royal Field Artillery serving in India and the South Africa wars in 1901. Leonard George was placed with the Chinese Labour Corps – using Chinese workers in non-combatant roles.

Ernest Samuel Dawkins remained a professional soldier; in 1893 he was stationed in Peckham in South London; in 1894 he married Mary Ann Dye from Peckham. The Dyes were

Hilda and Len

originally from Norfolk, and were grooms, coachmen, cabmen – horse people. Mary Ann had a different life, as she was a theatrical dresser including for Sir Seymour Hicks, a friend of W.S Gilbert (and Arthur Sullivan) and knighted in 1935. The world of the theatre would have been very exciting.

In Ernest Samuel Dawkins' Army records, he states in 1917 his next of kin, for funeral arrangements as his son-in-law, Randall Andrews. At this stage, none of his children were married so the older meaning of son-in-law applies, today it would be stepson. There are two recorded births for a Randall Andrews, the elder, and one for Randall Douglas Andrews, whose parents are "Annie Andrews, formerly Dye" and father "Randall Andrews", who emerges as Randall Hawkins Andrews, a bookmaker in 1892 and a theatrical agent in 1901, perhaps providing a connection for Mary Ann, the theatrical dresser. Clearly, Ernest Samuel took on the younger Randall when he married Mary Ann Dye in 1894. Randall Hawkins Andrews never married.

Ernest Samuel and Mary Ann's first child together, Leonard (Len) Godfrey Dawkins, came along in 1895 – he was to be my grandfather. It might be expected that Randall would take the Dawkins name, thus brushing over a dalliance, but that did not happen. Randall kept his name and Leonard was regarded as the eldest in the family. By 1911, Randall Douglas was a gunner in the Royal Garrison Artillery in Gibraltar and in 1920 he married and worked as a prison officer.

There are other children to Ernest Samuel who have been forgotten. The 1911 Census required householders to list their

Hilda and Len

children, including any who have died. Ernest Samuel had three; the first was Stuart Ernest Dawkins, born in 1897 and died in 1898. Stuart and his father were baptised on the same day, 24 March 1897. The other two were twins, Winifred Maud and Connie Irene, born in September 1908 and both died in October 1909. The Army records for Ernest Samuel mark him as suffering from secondary syphilis which is now associated with damage to both early and later children, likely to be the cause for the deaths of all three. My mother, Phyll, was named Phyllis Connie; but she never knew why she had this informal style of second name. It caused difficulty when officials expected it to be Constance. Her two aunts were dead and forgotten 12 years before she was born in 1921.

Ernest Samuel Dawkins had signed up to the Royal Artillery in Colchester in 1885 and the Army had moved him round the country. In 1898, Len and Randall were entered into the Campbell Street School in Westminster. In 1901, Len was with his parents at the barracks in Coventry and in 1911 they were all at 8 Halstow Road, Kensal Rise, London, except Randall, who had joined the Royal Garrison Artillery as a gunner. Each child had been born in a different place.

The move away from rural life brought the families of Hilda and Len into central London, where the very rich lived close by the very poor, who were employed to serve and so had to live nearby. In 1911, Len was a "worker", aged 15 in a provisions merchant – a grocer, probably Sainsbury's – the kind of work he continued for the rest of his life. Except, of course, he signed up for the Army in May 1915 in the Royal Field Artillery. That

Hilda and Len

took him to France in February 1917 where he stayed until July 1919 (apart from 3 weeks "furlough" back in Britain in 1918) and "admitted flu" in February 1919. The "flu" was probably what we now know as the 1918 pandemic of Spanish flu.

On 23 August 1919 he married Hilda at St Luke's Church, Kilburn; the witnesses were Randall (signing as Andrews) and Doris Ivy Dawkins, the youngest sister of Hilda. Bride and groom both gave their address as 340 Kilburn Lane, still in existence today with mildly elegant upper storeys, where they probably had a flat. They both liked a good time, dancing, snappy dressing and were pub regulars.

Phyllis Connie Dawkins was born on 23 January 1921. Len had masonic and business contacts: his customers in the heart of London were well-heeled and well-connected. His commanding officer in the Royal Artillery was 2nd Lieutenant Dennis Wheatley whose family owned Wheatley & Son of Mayfair, a wine business which did not thrive. He took up writing which was much more successful – a sequence of satanic stories emerged -"The Devil Rides Out" and even were produced as cinema successes – Len had a full set of the novels. Wheatley would have known of the Dawkins' aspiration for better accommodation and may have had a hand in their next move.

The family was then living at 23 Elgin Terrace, Paddington but by 1928 they had moved to 22 Carpenter Street Buildings in Mayfair – a building in which Hilda and Len remained for the next 32 years. They moved from one flat to another in the

Hilda and Len

buildings, by 1939 they were in No15 and after the war, they were in No 12. The attraction was, on the surface, obvious – this was the very heart of Mayfair then, as now, one of the most expensive and prestigious areas in Britain to call home. The church round the corner was St George's, Hanover Square. Built in the early 18th century, St George's was the church of Handel, who lived nearby in Brook Street; and it saw the weddings of Emma Hamilton, Shelley, Disraeli, George Eliot, Theodore Roosevelt and Asquith.

Film stars lived nearby, Berkeley Square was just round the corner, Mount Street, Carlos Place, Davies Street were the homes of the aristocracy and the world of glamour. You might go to one of the many nearby grand cinemas, see Michael Wilding in "The Courtneys of Curzon Street", "Spring in Park Lane" or "Maytime in Mayfair" each starring Anna Neagle and walk home through those very streets. You might see someone mentioned in the newspaper and pass them the very next day outside your front door. Film exists of Hilda and Len stepping out of the building, dressed to the nines, as smart as film stars. If this wasn't posh what was?

The reality was a little different. From the outside, it looked much like the other late 19th century, elegant, blocks in the area, many of which had stern uniformed doorkeepers. There was a laundry room on each floor, which also contained the bath, to be shared with two other flats on that level, as was the magnificent single lavatory mounted with a beautiful mahogany bench seat. There were two bedrooms, a parlour and a kitchen. Everyone smoked as did the coal fire which warmed the parlour. The flat

Hilda and Len

was rented from the Church Commissioners and the landlord did not invest much in it. The Church Commissioners sold off most of the Church's London property in the 1950s-60s.

But when you stepped out into the street, you felt a million dollars and there was a need to dress to match. By this time Len was working in selling fish, first in Sainsburys, then Gow's at Old Broad Street – involving a trip into the City. For this Len would dress in city gent style: black jacket, striped trousers, bowler hat and furled umbrella. His Fox's silk umbrella was taken for regular re-furling at James Smith & Sons in New Oxford Street. Once at the fish shop, he would change into the white coat and boots of the profession. Of course, the umbrella was never opened in rain. By 1958, the "Fish Trades Gazette" reported Len as working in Gow's for many years, photographed there showing off the smartly refitted shop.

Across the parlour fireplace hung an array of horse brasses, perhaps genuinely once worn by horses, and a small brass leg. There was a radiogram for playing 78 rpm records and special things were kept in a shiny, ebonised sideboard with red plush to make the drawers slide silently and keep out the dust. For selected visitors, there was a copy of the "most evil book in the world", as Len called it, a large volume of Adolf Hitler's manifesto "Mein Kampf", with a swastika embossed on the front. It was in German, printed in heavy German font, which no one could read but it was obviously satanic. One stood in awe.

Hilda and Len

Who would not be keen on cricket if they were members of the Marylebone Cricket Club? Sir Pelham Warner, presumably either a customer for game and fish or a frequenter of The Audley bar, put Len up for membership in 1960, Warner was chair of the Committee, which included Denis Compton, and the cricket correspondent of the Daily Telegraph.

Hilda worked too, her last job in London was as a book-keeper at Garrard, in Regent Street, then the holder of the Royal Warrant as Crown Jeweller of the UK.

In 1926, Hilda and Len's second child arrived, Donald Ernest, and then, in 1931, a second daughter, Eileen Ann.

Phyllis and Don attended Farm Street School, just a block away. It cannot have been easy, three children in a small flat. Eileen caught diphtheria when very young and went away for many weeks to a fever hospital. It seems probable that this was in September 1939 as the Register taken that month shows Hilda staying at 1 Vaughan Road, Biggleswade, while Len remained in Carpenter Street. In both entries in the 1939 Register, there is an adjacent entry "Officially Closed" which tends to mark a child. There are no entries for the children. There was a small fever hospital in Biggleswade. The large scale vaccination against diphtheria started in 1943 but before that the disease had been rife with 55,000 cases per year. Many years later Don said that while Eileen was in hospital (with every likelihood that she would not survive) he and Phyllis went into care (even though she was 18 years old – and almost certainly at work).

Hilda and Len

Don also spoke of other trouble. He suggested that Len had arranged for Phyllis to be taken on in the business in which he worked. A problem arose with some money in the till and Phyllis was dismissed. Don thought that Len had gone to the shop, in an angry mood, to protest against the peremptory action and was also summarily dismissed. It seems likely that this happened before the war, as Phyllis would have left school in 1935 and during the war she worked in the Ministry of Aircraft Production. However, the Fish Trades Gazette of 1958 includes a photograph of Len in his fishmongers "whites" suggesting that Len had been at Gow's for a good number of years.

Certainly, Phyllis earned praise during the war. She received a personal letter of 24 September 1943 from Lord Louis Mountbatten thanking her for "all the valuable and strenuous effort you have contributed to the running of the Combined Operations Headquarters Club". In August 1943 he had been appointed, by Churchill, as the Supreme Allied Commander South East Asia Command (SEAC) with promotion to acting full admiral.

Basingstoke

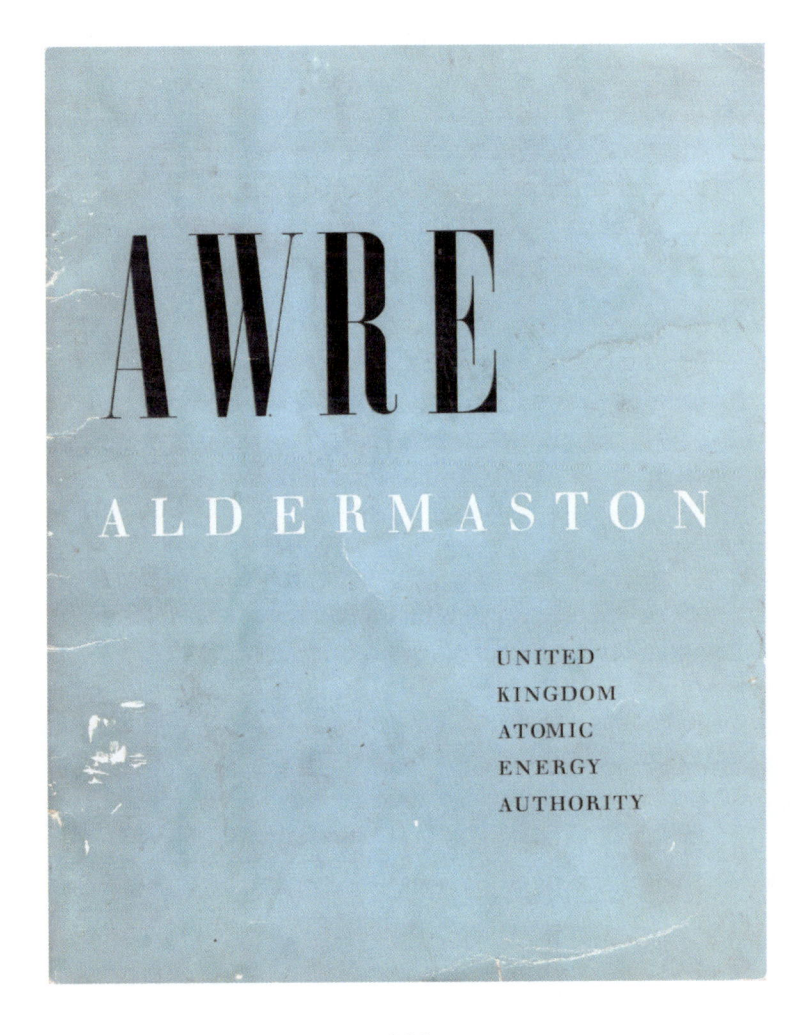

AWRE
ALDERMASTON

UNITED
KINGDOM
ATOMIC
ENERGY
AUTHORITY

Basingstoke

1932 the neutron was discovered at Manchester University by James Chadwick. In 1938 nuclear fission was discovered by Enrico Fermi; and in 1939 British scientists invented the atomic bomb which was then developed in partnership with scientists from the United States. The British and Americans exchanged nuclear information but did not initially combine their efforts; during 1940-41 the British Tube Alloys project was larger and more advanced but the Americans quickly caught up and took the lead. Without the British participation it would have taken longer to create the Hiroshima and Nagasaki bombs which brought the second World War to an end.

Most of this was not known outside a small circle of very senior people but there was terror deep in governments that the insane Adolf Hitler would gain access to these weapons. The general public across the world only came to know of this in August 1945, when the atomic bombs stopped Japan. Hitler had, in effect, already been defeated at the beginning of 1945 and he committed suicide on 31 May 1945.

By 1949 the USSR had demonstrated a nuclear weapon and a parallel industry of spying had been created. Very large investment was made in rapid developing and building ever more powerful nuclear weapons. The era of vast armies of squaddies tramping across mud deserts to wage war was expected to be over.

We left Eric Hewitt, on 26 October 1953, from the Ministry of Supply Atomic Weapons Research Establishment, Aldermaston, suggesting to Tom that he should apply for promotion to Senior

Basingstoke

Executive Officer. Clearly, Tom's capabilities were appreciated, as they had been at the Iron and Steel Corporation and then The Royal Ordnance Factory at Dalmuir, in Glasgow. That, and his wish to return Phyll to the familiar territory of the south of England, combined to give his career a real jump forward. The application was made.

Things moved quickly: on 2 November the Ministry of Supply offered posts at either Royal Ordnance Factory Burghfield or Aldermaston, both sites working to build and test the British atomic bomb. Houses were being built for staff at both sites. Christmas Eve 1953 brought a letter giving a start date at AWRE Aldermaston on Friday 1 January 1954. In classic civil service style this was then amended to Monday 4 January. There was obviously some pressure for speedy action.

It is hard to over-emphasise the urgency of the atomic project. The two atomic bombs dropped at Hiroshima and Nagasaki in August 1945 changed the whole nature of war. By August 1949 Russia had tested its first atomic bomb, having worked on it since 1939. In the early 1950s, there was huge concern that Russia, previously thought to be a primitive peasant country, could open a new war. Spies were being discovered on all sides so secrecy became a daily concern for anyone working on these projects. The urgent need was to design, test and build atomic bombs – to be ready in case the Soviets gained an upper hand. The atomic bomb project was top priority and top secret for the Government. Big armies and navies would be no match for a few nuclear bombs smaller than a Jeep but capable of wiping out large cities.

Basingstoke

At its peak, the British atomic bomb project employed about 24,000 people, in research and production, the vast majority brought from all over Britain to take forward the project which until then had been hidden. The need to house the influx, in largely rural areas, was met by building anew in many places, together with the schools and other facilities needed. This, of course, meant the creation of "atomic" communities. There was a standard way of doing this, established by the armed forces, so houses were similar in most new sites.

Phyll, Tom, Jan and I benefited from this. Early in 1954, the family entered a long, daffodil-bordered drive in Basing, Hampshire to take up temporary residence in a wing of "Sheldons" a large, rambling country house owned by Mrs Rattray. This was a temporary home but very exciting, being in deep, English countryside rather than the cold isolation of life in Cardonald. Basing was on the margins of Basingstoke, an old-fashioned Hampshire market town, still many years from its conversion to a bustling London overspill new town. Tom bought a car (having been taught to drive in Algiers during the war), and went off to work each day at Aldermaston.

Basingstoke was just an hour by train from Waterloo Station in London so Phyll could once again be with her family. Spring and summer in Hampshire were so good.

We left the rural dream of Basing in June 1954 and moved into 42 Stratfield Road in Basingstoke. This was on the Oakridge estate then just being completed – built entirely for United Kingdom Atomic Energy Authority (UKAEA) staff who would

Basingstoke

be working on nuclear weapons at Aldermaston. UKAEA was formed on 19 July 1954.

A mystery covers the name of the housing estate. In 1942 the US Government had taken over 24,000ha of land - a valley called "Oak Ridge" in Tennessee for the Manhattan project – which was to build the American atomic bomb.

No one is quite sure how the Basingstoke estate came to have almost the same name, it may have been an old name for the area but the same sense of urgency driving the American work pervaded the bomb project in Britain.

So new was our house that the back garden was a sea of bright red poppies, almost taller than Jan; as commonly grow on building sites; we made tunnels and lanes through the red mass. An infants school was built on the edge of the estate, reflecting that many residents would have young families.

Weekday mornings, all the men would travel to Aldermaston on fleets of buses and, gradually, in car pools, leaving wives to their own world. It was just far enough from Basingstoke town centre to mean that weekly shopping was the norm but soon traders began to arrive to sell from the back of their vans. Mary's van supplied sweets: wine gums, sherbet, Fox's Glacier mints for the smokers and Cadbury's chocolates. There were fish and meat vans too.

The children all walked to school and those of primary rather than infants age would walk to South View Primary School, in short trousers or grey pleated skirts and gaberdine raincoats, in

Basingstoke

all weathers and darknesses. The autumn walk across Farmer Snooks' field revealed the hand-making of sheaves and assembly into stooks as the harvest was gathered.

It looked like a normal local authority housing scheme but all the families worked at Aldermaston, so almost everyone knew everyone else. The streets were allotted by staff grade and promotion might mean moving house, even just a few hundred yards. There was a sense of mission, secrecy and, perhaps, concern about spies – so talk about work did not happen.

So what was the threat – who was the enemy?

It was only 20 years since Hitler had risen to world attention and only 40 years since the madness of the First World War broke out. In that time science and war had converged – so wars were to be won less by marching armies and more by science and technology. Radar and electronic coding and code-breaking were weapons. The structure of the atom was being refined week by week, by innocent scientists, not well-known figures, not quite yet "boffins". In 1933 Leo Szilard realised that a nuclear chain reaction was possible, where a neutron knocked into an atom and produced many more neutrons. A patent for a nuclear reactor was taken out by Szilard and Enrico Fermi in 1939 and by 1942 one was built in Chicago. It was realised that huge amounts of energy could be released – if done slowly this could generate electricity, if uncontrolled it was a bomb of astonishing power. So there was an odd split: nuclear reactors would provide cheap, clean power and a weapon that was almost too powerful to be used.

Basingstoke

The world was still reeling from bringing the war to an end. While Hitler had gone, the Communists were gaining strength. Russia, sometimes ally, sometimes enemy, could well mount an ideologically-based war – with an almost endless supply of troops – and what would they do if they had the bomb? So "reds under the bed" – communist infiltration – became the new enemy.

The work at Aldermaston was to build and test atomic bombs; led by William Penney, a mathematician, who had registered himself in September 1939 as available for scientific war work, but he had heard nothing for several months. In 1943 Penney was sent to join the team of British scientists at the Manhattan Project's Los Alamos Laboratory in New Mexico, where expertise on explosions and their effects was in demand. At Los Alamos Penney gained recognition for his scientific talents, and for his leadership qualities and ability to work in harmony with others. Within a few weeks of his arrival he was added to the core group of scientists making key decisions in the direction of the programme. Major General Leslie Groves, the director of the Manhattan Project, later wrote:

> "Throughout the life of the project, vital decisions were reached only after the most careful consideration and discussion with the men I thought were able to offer the soundest advice. Generally, for this operation, they were Oppenheimer, Von Neumann, Penney, Parsons and Ramsey."

Basingstoke

So William Penney was the British Oppenheimer. He worked in the American team that built the two atomic bombs used in 1945 and was present at the detonation of the second at Nagasaki. In 1950, the sleepy Berkshire airfield of Aldermaston was handed over for the development and construction of a British bomb – which proceeded quickly. The first test was on 16 October 1952 in the Monte Bello Islands off the west coast of Australia for which William Penney was knighted.

Tom at the feet of Sir William Penney

Basingstoke

It is not clear whether the atomic energy project actually required it but on 4 August 1954 Tom was commissioned into the Home Guard as a Second Lieutenant. The warrant provides that "you may hold any appointment in that force of such status as may be determined by Our Army Council to require commissioned rank". In short his instructions are to carry the weight of an officer.

On 10 September 1954, the Foreign Office issued a passport to Tom valid for the "British Commonwealth, all countries in Europe including the USSR, Turkey, Algeria, Azores, Canary Islands, Iceland and Madeira" – this appeared to be a standard list. Even so, many more exotic places were added in manuscript: "Indonesia, Lebanon, Egypt, Sudan, Syria, Iraq, Libya, Jordan, Bahrain, Saudi Arabia, Burma, Thailand, Vietnam, French , Spanish and Belgian possessions". Three days later, he was vaccinated against yellow fever, with more over the ensuing months and years for cholera, typhoid, paratyphoid and tetanus – clearly some significant wandering around the planet was to be expected.

On 13 October 1954 he was promoted to Senior Executive Officer in the Trials Planning Division led by Roy Pilgrim, deputy to Sir William Penney. On 6 April 1955, Tom flew into Mascot Airport, New South Wales, Australia and by 31 May 1955 he was back in Singapore flying back to Britain. The flights to and from Australia were on a Lockheed L-1049 Super Constellation with 4 engines driving propellers. It seated up to 102 passengers but could not manage the full distance in one hop, so broke the flight at Singapore. So what was he doing?

Basingstoke

Phyll knew little of what was happening, such were demands of security and secrecy. There were wisps of stories. One was that Tom had been to London to either collect or use the Great Seal of Britain to seal a document which would enable him, or perhaps the bearer, to arrive at Portsmouth Naval Dockyard to commandeer a frigate to take atomic material to Australia. The document was so valuable that he had been issued with a pistol to ensure that it would not be stolen; he and Phyll slept that night with the Seal or sealed document and the gun under their pillow. The next day he travelled to the dockyard to deliver his mission. No matter how thin or twisted the story may seem, it chimes with the demand for absolute loyalty and secrecy of the whole project.

He was in the core team at Maralinga, working directly with "Bill" Penney. In contrast to Oppenheimer, as he is portrayed today, Penney seems to have been an affable and approachable leader of whom Tom spoke warmly. The project started with a tented village and then wooden buildings were added, on a site 1500 miles from Sydney. Everything had to be provided from outside, at first by lorries on dirt tracks, then an airstrip was built. Water had to be found by drilling, kangaroos managed and the indigenous people found and helped to understand what was happening. Much of this was organised by Tom.

That first trip of almost 2 months in 1955 would have been focussed on the building of the Maralinga village, which came to be large, with many facilities to be provided for the scientific and engineering teams. There are many photographs of Tom with the Operation Buffalo team, including one where he

Basingstoke

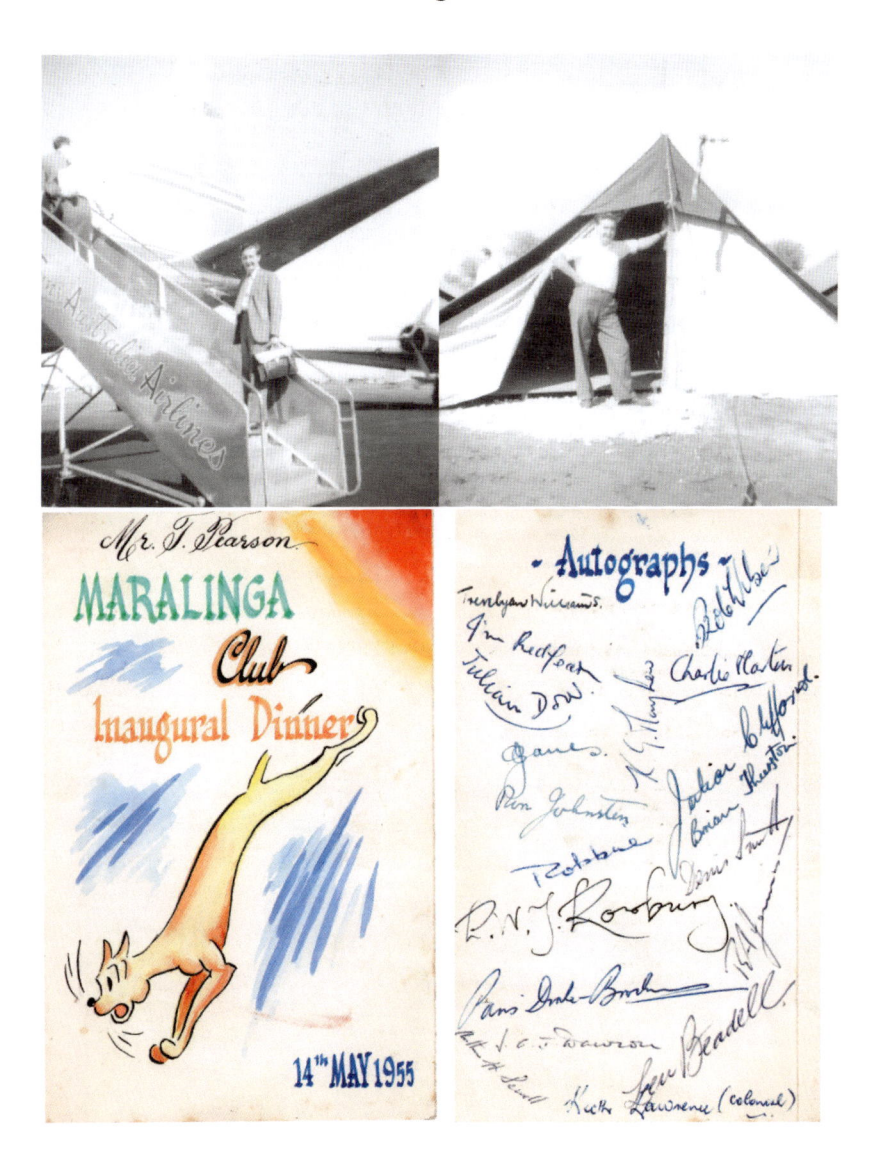

Basingstoke

Basingstoke

appears to be supervising a road construction, dressed in a tweed sports jacket – perhaps it was not always sweltringly hot.

A central and larger than life figure on site was Len Beadell, an Australian who had travelled across the territory, finding water sources and laying out access routes. Without him, the project would have been impossible. Not only was he the one and only man for the wilderness, he was a writer, also a well-known artist and cartoonist.

On 19 June 1956 Tom flew from London Airport into Sydney Kingsford Airport (Sydney had three airports) with many of the key Aldermaston team, including John Tomblin "physicist", and John Whitmore, the medical officer. Despite the secrecy the other passengers on the flight were ordinary folk from many backgrounds, travelling for all kinds of business and personal reasons. The National Museum of Western Australia has the Incoming Passenger Cards (Aircraft) for many of these flights, completed in manuscript.

The declared destination was the Weapons Research Establishment, Salisbury and the secret objective was the 4 test firings which made up Operation Buffalo.

27 September	"One Tree"	"on a tower"
4 October	"Marcoo"	"dry surface"
11 October	"Kite"	"air drop"
21 October	"Breakaway"	"tower"T

Basingstoke

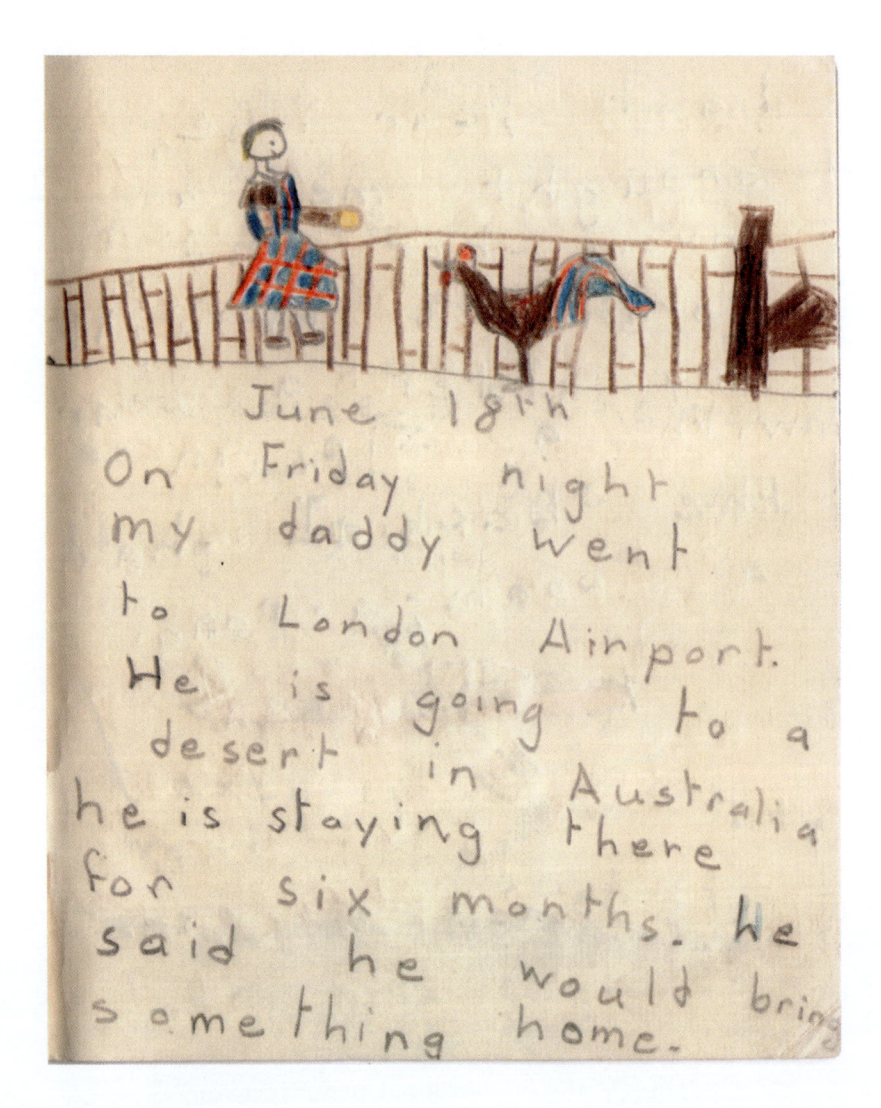

June 18th
On Friday night my daddy went to London Airport. He is going to a desert in Australia he is staying there for six months. He said he would bring something home.

Basingstoke

Last year he brought me a music-box and a torch. He brought my sister a bear with a zipp in the back. I had a boom-a-rang.

Basingstoke

Tom must have been present at all of these firings.

On 20 November 1956, setting off back to Britain, Tom arrived in Honolulu, under the authority of a "Non Immigrant Visa" issued by the American Consul in Sydney on 16 November for "unlimited applications for admission at United States ports of entry". The Commander of his flight issued a certificate that day under the authority of "King Neptune" to mark Tom's crossing of the Equator timed at 1520.

Much of the equipment used at Maralinga was built in Britain and the delicate items were packed for transit to Australia in large plywood cases containing Styrofoam blocks, invented in 1944 to protect fragile instruments. Once the contents were unpacked, the cases had little further use. However, some weeks after Tom's return a number of cases were returned to Britain containing artefacts. There were large red fossils, later distributed to Hampshire schools, and brass barrels – clearly intended to be fired from cannons, which provided novel containers for flower arranging.

Tom also found time for souvenir purchases: a koala night dress case for Jan and a realistic machine gun and musical box for me. Mulga wood ash trays, boomerangs, a snake stick, carved platters of homes in the outback, portraits of local people by Len Beadell topped off by "his and her" silver and gold silk brocade floor length dressing gowns – just the thing for a Basingstoke breakfast. More ash trays by the aboriginal potter Vande and a fragile woomera (a spear launcher) completed the swag.

Basingstoke

Another promotion came on 8 August 1956, to Chief Executive Officer. On 13 August, Phyll sent Tom a "Greetings Telegram" to Box No 1, Post Office, Maralinga, South Australia. She was congratulating him on this promotion which was approved for "January next" for 1957. A more formal telex appeared the next day from AWRE Aldermaston and on 31 December a grand letter arrived informing him that his annual salary from 1 January 1957 (that is the next day) would be £1,650, rising to £1,875. Tom did not return to Australia for the next phase of testing which would be Operation Antler, starting in the autumn of 1957

Tom never spoke of what he had seen. By this time, the world knew what had happened at Hiroshima and Nagasaki and that a conflict using such weapons was impossible. Even testing under the best of conditions was hazardous. I suspect that few working on the project, scientists, engineers, mathematicians, surveyors, had much idea of the danger they were in. They were mainly young, healthy young men and trusted the scientists they worked with.

In 1957, Nevil Shute published a novel "On the Beach" describing the consequence of a nuclear war – which ends with the last few survivors in Australia as the planet is engulfed in radiation. Even today, that possibility seems real – even though we have lived with it for over 75 years. The book was astonishing in 1957 but perhaps no more so than the launch that year by the USSR of the first orbiting man-made satellite. That happened just at the start of "The Sky at Night", a monthly TV programme on astronomy presented by Patrick Moore. Both

Basingstoke

startling events followed the less well published story in 1953 of the unravelling of DNA and its structure by Rosalind Franklin being confirmed by Crick and Watson some months later. Those first post-war years set the foundations for modern life – leading to better education and opportunities.

The secrecy on how to make a nuclear weapon which had been a feature of Aldermaston life was broken repeatedly and today the average modern physicist could sketch a design quickly. There were many benefits, but still significant dangers, in the civil use of nuclear knowledge and that became the function of the UKAEA.

There was a lot of concern about spies, communists and the like. The Russian spy Klaus Fuchs had worked at Harwell as a physicist, there was constant concern about "need to know" and this affected every family connected to the atomic projects. Behaviour that might lead to blackmail was a constant undercurrent. The secrecy probably also limited dissemination of information about the effects of radiation. It was only 10 years since the Hiroshima and Nagasaki bombs where the effects were initially seen as total obliteration. It was years before the insidious effects of low level radiation were appreciated. The current goal was to ensure that nuclear war would be rendered impossible by arming all sides equally – the Americans talked of "mutually assured destruction" – MAD was the acronym. Escalation was one outcome.

In 1958 Tom was promoted to being a "Banded" officer so we moved from 42 Stratfield Road (a 3 bedroom house) to, a large

Basingstoke

4 bedroomed house at 6 Sutton Road where all the senior staff lived. We had a long garden which ended in mature trees, separating us from the austere buildings of Queen Mary's School for Boys, a traditional grammar school taking only boys who had passed the 11-plus examination.

Two doors down was John Tomblin, the superintendent of the testing programme at Maralinga, whose sons were our

Basingstoke

playmates. Further along was John Corner CBE, the mathematician, who was the senior theoretician for the bomb. Across the road was Ieuan Maddock who became Chief Scientist at the Ministry of Defence (and was knighted for it).

Living in such a community encouraged a can-do attitude and worship of the scientists, engineers and mathematicians who were our neighbours. The wider world was also keen on making and doing. Doing your own home decoration was encouraged by new television series. In 1957, Barry Bucknell started his "Do-it-Yourself" TV series – Tom acquired a good set of tools in order to follow the instructions.

On Saturday mornings all four of us would go in the car to Basingstoke, then a sleepy Hampshire market town.

Tom would dress casually for the weekend in a tweed sports jacket, Clydella shirt, woollen Munrospun tie and beige cavalry twill trousers with good brogues. He might well wear a cap and carry his pipe in the coat pocket. The primary goal was Ody's grocer shop – this had been a bank and carried the style that Phyll had known in Hannells of Mayfair, which had been Hilda's local shop. This was the great centre, presided over by Charles Ody behind a long mahogany-topped counter. At one end, near the window, was a huge red machine with a vase-shaped hopper on top into which your coffee beans, chosen from a bewildering array of troughs, would be poured from a bright metal scoop. All the metal parts were shiny grey metal as found on aircraft hulls and there were various controls to be set. Then the power was turned on and immediately the shop was filled

Basingstoke

with the aromatic vapour of ground coffee, sort of burnt, kind of sweet, not immediately attractive but clearly appetising. The powerful motor ran for a minute or so as the beans clattered from hopper to hod. The hod was also red metal with a handle and a spout. The coffee was poured into an upright, sturdy brown paper bag, the top folded over twice and sealed with a sticky label. "There you are, madam what else can I get you?"

Looking round the shop, it was hard to imagine what was in the jars, boxes, packets: how did you know what to ask for?

"A pound of the best butter please". The centre of attention moved to the other end of the counter where stood a substantial person armed with a pair of square ping-pong bats. She wore a white cap, and beamed protectively at a huge, oily, luridly yellow cube – she lifted a T-shaped handle, tethered with a fine steel wire, and pulled it down on the cube. Two swift movements and a pound of butter stood ready on a special square of grease-proof paper. The ping-pong bats were used to mould the pound into a brick shape and "that's 12 ounces" "A little more please" and the brick was extended with a smidgeon from the cube, re-moulded and the grease-proof folded over into a neat package.

The shop was beginning to fill with women carrying wicker baskets, all keen to fill with similar hand-made items. Eggs, Lea and Perrins sauce, BeRo flour, sherry "sweet or dry?" chocolate biscuits. The lists were fumbled and adjusted continuously, everyone patiently waiting their turn to be served by one of the many, friendly and helpful assistants. Once we had made our

Basingstoke

selection the final act was to pay and ask that the assembled groceries be delivered late in the day. Mr Ody knew where we lived; we paid in cash (later by cheque) and moved on down the street to repeat the performance in the butcher, and the fruiterer. Later in the week a visit was made to the fishmonger and game dealer, where the knowledge acquired from our family connections in that trade were demonstrated.

But Saturday morning had to continue with the stately procession along the High Street: Boots the Chemist, right next door to Timothy Whites which sold almost the same things. Occasionally we would "pop in" to Vernon Griffiths, where Mr Vernon would advise on a hearth rug or a set of walnut occasional tables. The atmosphere here was of sacred calm and a strong scent of wool carpets and wax polish. Two small paintings of flowers, oil on wood, remain with the family.

Otherwise we would often meet friends and neighbours, almost exclusively "atomic" people. As grown-ups were prone to do, there were long, boring and incomprehensible conversations while children waited patiently. If the children were from our schools there might be conversation at their level, sharing the embarrassment of meeting or displaying sullen silence. Sometimes we would meet people like the Paices: Dennis worked at Aldermaston and Mrs Paice was Jan's infant school teacher – arrangements for afternoon tea visits might be made.

As we returned to the car, excitement grew: sweet shops appeared and small purchases of Maynard's wine gums could made (Jan liked sherbet fountains). For me there were two shop

Basingstoke

windows which demanded regular examination. An optician displayed optical instruments, all vastly expensive but achievable after many months of saving. A small microscope, with glass slide and tweezers, was the first. At last I could see, live, the things illustrated in The Observer's books on pond life, mosses and lichens, butterflies, moths and other insects. The microscope cost £2,19 shillings and 6 pence. A small refracting telescope followed. There was also a stamp shop so I was able to add to my small collection, but when I finally saved enough for a £5 Penny Black that brought collecting to a close.

The highlight of Saturday morning was ten minutes looking in the window of the shop that sold electrical appliances: vacuum cleaners, wireless sets, radiograms and television sets, which could receive both the BBC and Independent Television. The most fascinating items were the tape recorders with microphones. Grundig was the leading make; they were German, had the highest reputation and were expensive. Much weekly discussion focussed on wondering what they could be used for.

Finally, there was the visit to the library, returning last week's books and choosing anew. Phyll and Tom always chose novels: R F Delderfield, Nevil Shute, C P Snow. As they were allowed 4 books each and never managed more than 2 a week, I was able to borrow 6 each week, always science or electronics.

Then home in time for lunch and to await Ody's delivery.

Basingstoke

The Dawkins visited several times with their new families, The men would wander round at Sunday lunchtime to take a pint at "The Soldier's Return" pub – renamed by Tom as "The Sailor's Retreat" (or was it the other way round?).

I passed the 11-plus exam.

Passing – or not passing – the 11-plus was a defining moment in many lives with education viewed as a passport to success. The 11-plus examination was identified in the minds of parents as ensuring "he's going to get a good job".

Tom had seen the benefit of education from his few years at Bede Collegiate School which had lifted him into the Civil Service and now his neighbours and work colleagues were at the highest levels of scientific and academic achievement. So there were grounds for parental ecstasy. The Headmaster of South View Primary School, Jimmy Gardner, had telephoned Tom on the morning of the results. Tom immediately went out to buy a brand new Ferguson reel-to-reel tape recorder., which I had ogled weekly on our Saturday morning trips into Basingstoke and was waiting for me when I came home.

In September 1960, I started at Queen Mary's School for Boys which overlooked our house – at the foot of the garden. That introduced the novelty of boys not from "atomic" families, whose fathers did not take two-month holidays in Australia and what they did was not a taboo topic. A brand new car, a Ford Consul, appeared (this replaced a Ford Popular which had been bought from Ken Wood, who lived in Woking and had

Basingstoke

developed and marketed the Kenwood Chef food mixer) and a glossy Philips stereo radiogram. Our kitchen was equipped in 1961 with a Hoover Keymatic washing machine, thought to be the first in Hampshire and very expensive (£2500 today). Tom's hard work and now significant salary had produced tangible results.

Although Tom could now acquire luxuries he took little interest in them. Looking back, he spent money out of affection for Phyll. For example, the radiogram arrived with two long-playing records: "The King and I" and "South Pacific" – films they had seen on release. In London, the cinema had been the best night out – with new films appearing every week but that all stopped with marriage and family. Tom treated himself to a 7 inch single of Eartha Kitt singing "Just An Old Fashioned Girl" but he never played it. The radio would be on in the kitchen with "Children's Favourites" presented by Uncle Mac on Saturday mornings and Sunday lunch was always prepared with a background of "Two-Way Family Favourites" – one of the most popular programmes, rooted in connecting families with troops abroad.

Our television sets were rented – weekdays, the BBC 9 O'clock News marked the end of the evening and winter weekend afternoons were spent watching a "good picture". Reading novels was Tom's main recreation, before sleeping for the night – lights out well before 10pm. Mornings started at 6am with shoe polishing by Tom of his and our shoes. The army life might have given him this routine, I suspect there is a gene for early

Basingstoke

rising as I have always woken and been at my best well before 6am.

Tom was at his best with people but he didn't play golf, or go to the pub, or watch sport of any kind. He did join Masonic lodges but almost certainly only as an adjunct to business or work. Even so when there were difficulties with the trades unions he was happy to set up a bowls match with the management and down a pint or two in the "Club". In Basingstoke, all our neighbours and friends were "atomics" with almost no social contacts in the wider community. Looking back, this may have been because of security concerns – spies were a "real and present danger". That confined life also suited Phyll, who often appeared shy and clearly looked to Tom for protection. She made few, if any, friends – there were no "girls nights out". Most of our neighbours were university graduates of distinction – Phyll may have been reluctant to talk of her and Tom's "humble" origins. She was always keen to refer to her life in London – very few people would have been brought up just round the corner from Berkeley Square or been married in a society church like St George's, Hanover Square. She lived a life drawing on Tom's and her children's successes but sought little for herself.

Tom threw himself into a new life, joining the Parent-Teacher Association of the primary school at South View and leading a project to build a swimming pool there. Parents, of course, were able to swim there too and Tom did. Then, on 15 February 1962, Jimmy Gardner, Headmaster of South View Primary School, wrote to Tom to thank him for his three years of work on the

Basingstoke

swimming pool and the Parent Teacher Association. A month later we moved north.

The 1963 Partial Nuclear Test Ban Treaty banned atmospheric testing but in 1962 Tom had already moved on to the management of the UKAEA civil nuclear facilities. His skill at getting projects started was used in setting up the Southern Works Organisation to provide common services across the many UKAEA sites in the south.

Tom was chatty, affable, always ready to chat. He could be conspiratorial but also kept secrets secret. Not only that, he was scrupulously honest. His responsibilities at UKAEA Southern Works, covered all UKAEA sites and this included catering. He came home one autumn day excited about a deal done that day with a supply of turkeys for Christmas at a very advantageous price. His team had found that with the advent of machine feather-plucking there were occasional machine errors, with a leg being plucked off rather than a feather. This rendered the carcase unsaleable on the retail market but fine for works canteens.

On Christmas Day, we opened the front door, to find a large hamper on the doormat, with a card of appreciation from the turkey supplier. Tom closed the front door and instructed that the package was not to be touched – we had to use the back door. A "clearly worded" call was made the supplier, asking for this token of gratitude, or bribe, to be removed and nothing more would be said. And so it was.

Basingstoke

One afternoon, in Basingstoke, the telephone rang. Phyll answered; it was Tom asking her to prepare for an extra mouth at dinner that night. She was always a bit shy and was now a little thrown as Tom explained that Fred Lee MP, Minister of Power (and therefore the Minister for nuclear power) was at a loose end that evening. Quite how that went is not clear, a chicken was roasted and some cans of beer opened.

Tom acquired a wide circle of Aldermaston and Basingstoke friends and there were frequent visits, often on a Sunday afternoon, where two families would get together for tea. In some ways these trips were more to get Phyll out of the house (and to make use of the car) than any real social purpose. Eventually Tom decided to host a Christmas party, inviting perhaps 100 guests for an evening. Phyll baulked at preparing for this - probably with shades of the Glasgow problems – and Tom brought in caterers. He liked to socialise and the Oakridge estate, for all the concerns about secrecy and security, was a ready-made social circle. Unsupervised playing in the street was safe. Walking to school in the dark across fields raised no concerns – there were no strangers.

In addition, for such men, the Masonic Lodge, clubs for men to meet for "self improvement" was a social step up. Tom's and Phyll's fathers were both Masons so for Tom joining a lodge was an obvious step. There was an air of mystery and secrecy, for those not in the know, "funny handshakes", initiations, aprons and more which added zest to a monthly get-together. Tom had been admitted as a Life Member to a lodge in Glasgow: "The Lodge Renfrew County Kilwinning No 370" on 28 May 1953 –

Basingstoke

just 3 months before he applied for compassionate transfer from the Royal Ordnance Factory at Dalmuir. Clearly the years 1954 -1956 were taken up with the Maralinga tests but by 1958 he is recorded as a Founder Member of The Vyne Lodge, which held its Consecration at the Masonic Hall, Basingstoke, on 9 October that year. Sir Charles Chute, 1st, and only, Baronet, of Vyne House, had given permission for the name and his crest to be used. The Lodge held its meetings in the Wheatsheaf Hotel in Basingstoke – other Founder Members probably came from Aldermaston.

As children, Jan and I delighted in a Sunday morning car trip to the woods of The Vyne, a secret place where wild flowers and insects abounded – creating an interest fuelled by "The Observers" book series.

In 1922, a new edition was published of "The Children's Encyclopaedia", originally produced as a fortnightly part-work by Arthur Mee. Over 800,000 copies of the material in the 10 volumes had been produced since it began in 1908. Arthur Mee was "trying to encourage the raising of a generation of patriotic and moral citizens". It is not a classic encyclopaedia, with alphabetic entries. Instead, it is a sequence of 12 subject areas repeated over and over in short chapters which made it a readable rather than just a reference work.

In many ways the encyclopaedia expressed pride for Great Britain and its empire. his was presented in a moderate and liberal way in many areas: other "races", although inferior according to the text, were to be treated with respect, and

Basingstoke

imperialism was justified only if it improved the lot of its subjects. At a time when the relation between science and religion was controversial, the encyclopaedia supported evolution based on Darwin's views.

A set of this encyclopaedia was brought into the Pearson home in Sunderland. It is not clear when, how or for whom. Tom's signature appeared in one volume – and he clearly knew the volumes well. Around 1957, 8 of these volumes arrived in Basingstoke – to Jan and me this was done without ceremony. Did they come by post, were they collected from a far-off place or delivered by someone in the Pearson family? Whatever the answer, these books became a central component of our childhood. The elegantly bound books seemed to cover all aspects of life from "Things to Make and Do", through Greek and Roman history to the building of a "modern" house (Arthur Mee's own) and the wonder of the world in modern engineering of the Forth Railway Bridge. There was poetry, music, photographs – an endless parade of fascinating ideas.

A couple of years later, another parcel arrived containing Volumes 9 and 10. The last volume was the Index – so now anything and everything could be found with ease. Even now more than 100 years after their publication, these volumes present a comprehensive basis for an informed life.

In Basingstoke, there were many weekly deliveries of comics and more. I had "The Eagle" and "The Children's Newspaper" (connected to the Arthur Mee encyclopaedia); Jan had others for her age.

Basingstoke

The encyclopaedia had probably pandered to Tom's inquisitive and sensitive nature. Arnett was 11 years and Eileen 7 years older than him – so by the time Tom was 8 his elder siblings were close to adulthood and certainly working. Even Amy, 2 years older than Tom, may have been a lively teenager – so Tom was free to study as he wished, and he did.

When the first parcel of volumes arrived in Basingstoke, Jan and I did not know of our relatives in Sunderland. We knew, and saw regularly, Len and Hilda, who were only 50 miles away in London. There were trips by train to London; we became familiar with the sites on the train route, skirting round the astonishing Battersea Power Station, just before arriving at Waterloo. A short taxi ride took us to Carpenter Street, where lived "Nana and Grandad". Day trips to London were frequent, familiar and fun. Fairly soon, these trips were made by car, that Ford Popular, – perhaps less fun as the traffic built up on the A30 between Basingstoke and London. Don and Audrey had married in March 1950 followed by a honeymoon in Paris. As a wedding present, perhaps, perhaps to himself, Don had acquired a 9.5mm ciné camera – for Paris movies. He made films of me at 3 years old playing on the steps of the Albert Memorial just across the road from their flat just along from the Royal Albert Hall. So there was a tight, warm relationship with the Dawkins family.

By the late 1950s, the owners of the Carpenter Street Buildings recognised the value of the site, the poor return from their tenants and the need for substantial modernisation. By 1959, only 8 flats showed as occupied on the Electoral Roll and no further lets were made. Len was 65, with only the State Pension

Basingstoke

in prospect. Len and Hilda were virtually penniless. The landlord started to put on pressure. The time had come for change.

Tom was at the centre of the change. In 1960, Len and Hilda came to live in Basingstoke – they had liked the place, especially "The Soldier's Return" pub on the edge of the Oakridge estate. Tom arranged for Len to be employed as a messenger at Aldermaston – his birthday was 7 July and this was a new beginning, but not for long: he died six weeks after the move. In the previous months, Phyll and Tom had been looking at places for Len and Hilda to live and had settled on a ground floor maisonette, just being built, with a small, south facing garden. The upper flat was occupied by a quiet, academic civil servant who took the train every day to Whitehall. Tom bought the flat with a loan and each week we would drive across town to collect the rent, with the details included in the Rent Book. The rent was covered by a social security payment. The rent went to pay off Tom's loan.

After Len's death Hilda took as job as a book keeper in a paper works. There she stayed until Phyll and Tom moved north and she wished to move nearer to her other daughter, Eileen, and her husband Ron, now prospering in Maidstone. That deal was done – Ron took on a new loan to pay for a flat in Maidstone, releasing Tom from his deal. Hilda died just 3 months before her 100th birthday, in Woodhall Spa in 1997 where Eileen and Ron had moved on his retirement.

Basingstoke

I remember being about 9 years old and Tom giving me one of his Clarnico mints – a shocking, strong taste something like Vim or Ajax, violent bleaching and scouring powders, guaranteed to shift hard water stains from anything. I knew I wanted to vomit but was too polite. He moved on to Fox's Glacier Mints, like little glass loaves of bread for slicing that started frosty but went transparent with sucking. They had sharp corners and a rounded top. They weren't too bad – but that feeling ended when Fox's Glacier Fruits appeared – just chemical colours.

Salvation came with After Eight Mints, made exotic by each wafer having an individual, dark, crackly, paper envelope. Dark chocolate, that didn't taste of chocolate and a soppy mint-ish filling, much like tooth paste. In fact, peppermint achieved great importance for no obvious reason – everyone had them.

Then in 1962 the Royal College of Physicians concluded

> "Cigarette smoking is a cause of lung cancer and bronchitis, and probably contributes to the development of coronary heart disease and various other less common diseases."

This was reported in The Times, which I had just started reading. Tom had introduced Phyll to smoking, to "keep him company"; she started with "elegant" little pink boxes of du Maurier and later Sobranie Black Russian, with gold bands. Tom was coughing his way through Players "Senior Service". It was a dark day when I, aged 12, suggested that based on the Royal

Basingstoke

College advice, Tom and Phyll should give up smoking. It was the cause of anger.

So smoking, with that reek and filth of the paraphernalia, continued. At Christmas, there were specials, like Hamlets. Well into the 1970s any social occasion would open with offering "have one of mine" and in offices meetings would start with universal lighting up.

But if you never started, every encounter was marred by the risk of smoking, and worse, the social stigma of "No thanks, I don't". It was an easy step to see that the popularity of mints came mainly from their power to overwhelm the stink and vile after-taste. Polos, Murray Mints, Fox's – all of them thrived from cigarettes. The array of mint-flavoured sweets continued and as smoking made your mouth dry a "fag" inevitably demanded an accompanying "cuppa".

That said there was style to be had. Tom took up smoking a pipe, with a whole new array of requisites: Dutch tobaccos that had a caramel tang, special pouches for the "baccy" and pipe, long matches, exotic tamping and scraping tools and twisted hands from trying to ignite with a petrol lighter (another requisite) and then the special hacking, retching cough which could be soothed only by a fresh pipe. The final fun came one day when Tom was driving the family in the car and his tweed sports jacket pocket caught fire, as he had failed to put the pipe "out" before setting off.

Basingstoke

But nothing can surpass the nausea of coming down in the morning to a room full of cigarette corpses and the ineradicable reek.

Basingstoke

Early days in 42 Stratfield Road

1955

Tom, Don Dawkins, Audrey Dawkins, Phyll, Eileen Simpson, Christopher Dawkins, Jan

Photograph by Ron Simpson

Basingstoke

Lymm

The Cross, Lymm.

We had moved to Cheshire where Tom would become the Group Efficiency Services Officer for the UKAEA based at its HQ at Risley. The atomic bomb world fell away and power reactors and science were the new focus. We would live in the village of Lymm in a high quality house bought for the purpose by the Authority – we moved in over Easter 1962. Risley did not have the level of security demanded at Aldermaston but a small enclave of UKAEA houses had been built in Appleton, Warrington, presumably there were no vacancies there – and 318 Higher Lane, Lymm was obtained. Nostalgically, Tom

Lymm

made a name plate for the house, "Sheldons" recalling the first house in Basing. He would drive to work in the large office complex that had been built on the former RAF Padgate site. I went to Lymm Grammar School - then a large co-educational selective grammar school; Jan went to primary school in Lymm and then to the private Culcheth Hall School for Girls in Altrincham.

Basingstoke had been idyllic – endless days of playing in sun, roaming the countryside, sliding down into chalk pits and coming home covered in white dust. We were within walking distance of schools and Basingstoke town centre. Even when it rained we were protected by navy blue belted gaberdine raincoats. I wore with pride my black grammar school cap, adorned with a silver metal badge. There must have been bad days – but they are forgotten. There must have been bad weather but not for long.

The north of England was different. These were the last days before smokeless fuels so smog, which Monet had recorded in London was still present. It was possibly worse as even in rural Cheshire, the industrial north was not far away. Smog is an evil weather condition where smoke from coal fires mixes with fog to produce a dense, yellow, damp blanket. Smog came to Lymm. One night Tom and I were out in the car and encountered smog a couple of miles from home. If the headlights were on, the glare reflected by the toxic soup of gas blinded the driver. Eventually, I had to walk in front to indicate where the road went, with Tom driving on sidelights. It seemed a very long way breathing the choking, sulphurous effluvia.

Lymm

We were mid-way between Altrincham and Warrington. Altrincham was in its last days of being a sleepy, independent market town, in the foothills of the monstrous Manchester. The ring of millionaire footballer villages had yet to be populated: Wilmslow, Knutsford, Alderley Edge, Hale, Mobberley, even Lymm were aspiring but not taken over. It had a train station, going direct to Manchester, Oxford Road. A bus from Lymm and a train could have you in the city in no more than 90 minutes.

Warrington was at its most desperate. The Mersey ran through it, often completely coated in grey foam from the soap works and other industries. It was smoky, and full of traffic; not pleasant. The big stores were here so visits for school uniforms and shoes were regular. Its railway stations took you to Liverpool and Chester. But it was an important Saturday morning destination as it had a record shop, with hooded listening booths, so armed with 6 shillings and 8 pence you could buy the latest 7inch single. The bus was 5 shillings return. So for £1 (20 shillings) you could take a bus to Warrington, buy two of the latest Tamla Motown singles and still have change. Petrol was cheap too 4 gallons (18 litres) for £1. On the way to Warrington you could stop off at the Latchford Army Surplus shop selling mysterious electronic stuff.

Nights out in Liverpool (via Warrington) and Manchester (via Altrincham) were feasible. The D'Oyly Carte performances of *The Mikado* and *The Gondoliers* took me to Liverpool in 1966 and the Four Tops came on in Manchester in early 1967.

Lymm

Lymm schools and church provided many opportunities for Tom to involve himself in village life. He became a sidesman at Lymm Church, joined the PTA Committee at the grammar school, and took part in fund-raising for a roof for the school swimming pool.

Although the house in Higher Lane was smart and comfortable, it was relatively isolated, leaving Phyll on her own for much of the time – so for a while she took a job as a school secretary in Mobberley. Probably to avert any return of the difficulties in Glasgow, in early 1966, Tom bought a newly-built house, 1 Grove Rise, the first house he had owned, in the very centre of Lymm, clearly intending to become a permanent citizen in the village.

Shortly after moving we had a visit from an advertising agency, keen to use the house in an advertisement for electricity. Our new, white, Ford Corsair, bench seats, column gear change, was parked elegantly outside. Models posed against the sleek vehicle, photographs taken, fee paid – but the advertisement didn't appear once the gas-fired central heating was noticed.

Tom was fun. As my friends and I got older, our lives and interests expanded. Alcohol was difficult to secure until you could pass for 18 years of age. One of my friends, John, discovered that the landlord of The Bear's Paw public house at High Legh was happy to recognise the maturity of customers and supply glasses of port and lemon or Guinness. At closing time John would cycle unsteadily home but realise that he could not go straight home in that state. Instead, he came to our house,

Lymm

in the centre of Lymm, where Tom would give him a warm reception, coffee and an alibi.

Equally he was tolerant. As my technical expertise grew, in 1966 I converted a valve radio to be a medium wave transmitter. John climbed a tree at the end of our garden to attach the long wire aerial. I broadcast music for some days until one evening Tom came home from the office saying that I had been asked to play a request on my pirate radio station. The truth came out and the aerial came down.

Very occasionally, Tom would become nostalgic about food. He announced that his mother used to bake bread and he would make some. The kitchen was cleared, the doors sealed and he got on with it. He was on his own, having procured yeast in Lymm village, and what seemed like hours passed. Positive signs: after a lot of swearing B*** and D*** (nothing stronger) the house began to fill with that fresh bread smell.

After what seemed a long time, the kitchen door opened, revealing a scene of devastation with flour everywhere and many pans and utensils needing attention. But there was bread: a dozen or so very white, torpedo shape, rolls. Of course, we had to try them. To be honest they were delicious once you risked teeth in biting through the crust. His mother justifiably called them "tuffies" but that was and is a Sunderland term for these.

Tom was then ejected from Phyll's pristine kitchen.

Lymm

Food nostalgia extended to European cuisine; Tom's year in Naples had given him a taste for pasta. Again the culinary operating theatre was set up and spaghetti Bolognese was made. I think by then I had decided that pasta was vile but the aromas were good and Tom felt that he had proved his point.

The spaghetti exercise was not repeated.

In late September 1967, I "went up" to the "Victoria University of Manchester" to read physics, starting on the day that BBC Radio 1 began. Meanwhile Tom had revived his French speaking by helping with emerging twinning of Lymm with Meung sur Loire, a town near Orleans. He surprised people as he was reasonably fluent in French but with a pied-noir accent, having used French daily in Algiers, rather than France.

Lymm

Reay Beach

The list of the best beaches in Britain must include virtually all those on the northern coast of Caithness and Sutherland. The sands are white and vast – and face onto the Pentland Firth. In mid-summer, the sun never fully sets and in mid-winter it barely appears. Caithness, now called the Flow Country, is a huge green triangle of peat moss – populated by deer and plants which eat insects, and fewer than 20,000 people. It is ringed on the horizon by the mountains of Sutherland and across the Firth the islands of Orkney are close by. There is haar here too, although the wind is often too strong for it to linger. The whole area is now ringed by the North Coast 500 route which used to be a relentless single track road with passing bays.

The coast contains a number of mysterious establishments, including the United States Navy. The most obvious is Dounreay, which started as a war-time aerodrome and in the 1950s experimental nuclear installations were made. There was a fear of a nuclear accident and this was the most remote part of Britain, although if radioactive material were to be released, it would reach the cities of northern England within a few hours.

In September 1969, Tom was appointed to the Dounreay management team and the family moved from Lymm into 3 Castlegreen Road, Thurso, a house almost identical to 6 Sutton Road in Basingstoke – carpets for one would fit the other. The windows were smaller, still no double-glazing; the kitchen had a Rayburn cooker which also heated one or two radiators. The island of Hoy could be seen from the windows upstairs.

But like Oakridge in Basingstoke, there was a strong community of "atomics", some we knew from Aldermaston and Risley. The "atomics" dominated the place, not quite overwhelming the Georgian formal layout of the town. Everyone worked at Dounreay, so every morning there was an exodus to the site about 10 miles away. On arrival, in October, almost immediately there was a snowfall which blocked the road to Dounreay for 3 weeks. That meant that Tom, part of the senior management team, could not get to work.

There were constant visitors by nuclear "royalty" such as Glenn Seaborg, the chairman of the United States Atomic Energy Commission in 1971 who had worked on the Manhattan Project, the American equivalent to the work done in Britain at Aldermaston. I was able to visit experimental sites, marching through the beginnings of the seemingly vast Prototype Fast Reactor (PFR) cooled by 1,500 tonnes of liquid sodium. Sodium catches fire if exposed to air so needs to be managed carefully. There was a sodium rig at Risley: one Sunday morning Tom was called out as there had been an incident with a sodium release affecting a herd of cows, with a very angry farmer. The farmer had to be placated by the purchase of his whole herd, which could not be saved. Tom did a quick, quiet deal and life carried on.

Reay Beach

The Queen Mother spent summers at the Castle of Mey about 15 miles along the coast and frequently drove herself into "town" to meet her friend Miss Calder, owner of the J. Miller-Calder auction house and antique business. She also kept "refreshments" in her office to which the two ladies would retire. The other way along the coast would take you to Thurso Castle, a seat of John Sinclair, Viscount Thurso. Tom and Phyll would occasionally be invited to dine with the Sinclairs – and Tom went salmon fishing on the Thurso river with their ghillie (the same ghillie looked after the Queen Mother when she fished. Phyll and Lady Thurso would drive around the town doing charitable works together.

In Thurso, Tom borrowed a ghillie from Lord Thurso and went fishing up the Thurso river. After a day, a triumphal Tom showed off the decent-sized salmon he had caught, under the "supervision" of a tweed-clad expert. No one fancied cleaning this large creature but it had to be done before freezing. Although Phyll's father, Len Dawkins, had been a fishmonger and we had his smoked salmon slicing knife, she did not fancy the job. I did it, which is a much easier exercise than might be supposed – two swift incisions revealed the entire entrails which came away in one piece. Plenty more wild salmon was consumed in Thurso but bought fully prepared by a fishmonger.

And one day standing in an icy Highland river was enough.

The train from Manchester to Thurso then took about 18 hours, including 5 hours for the 150 miles from Inverness to Thurso – three trains a day. The "London" papers would arrive about

Reay Beach

4pm, the next day. On Fridays, Nobles, the purveyors of fruit and vegetables, would receive their stocks from the south, including the exotic green pepper. Weekends were filled with dinner parties, often opening with the modern delicacy of stuffed green peppers.

On New Year's Eve, first footing would consume the whole town, with great clusters of young people, in various stages of merriment, parading from party to party all night. On Mid-Summers Eve, a golf match would begin at 11pm and play would continue through the night. But the nearest Marks and Spencer was in Aberdeen and there were only two television channels – the "colour" programmes were blocked by the hills at Dunbeath on which the Duke of York was mysteriously killed in a plane crash in 1942.

A group of some student friends came by car for New Year 1971 – the days of the Ibrox football disaster. One trip home from Manchester was made overnight in a friend's Singer Chamois (a posh Hillman Imp) – coming over the tops of hills of Sutherland dawn broke to show miles of valleys filled with haar – a deep sea of perfect white glistening, level mist into which we gradually descended.

Only a few months later, I graduated and returned home to find Tom in Inverness Hospital having major abdominal surgery. I was booked in for minor nasal surgery so briefly we were there together. The Thurso years were over; the whole family returned to Lymm and Tom and Jan to work at Risley. In late

Reay Beach

1971, the family moved into 12 Greenwood Road, Lymm, just up the hill from our previous house at 1 Grove Rise.

In 1972 I started a business, based from home, doing electronics: small TV and hi-fi repairs, and some teaching about electricity in primary schools, while I looked for a first job after graduation. Tom was still recovering from his surgery but working at Risley. Early on I applied to the BBC to be a trainee in programme production (on the basis of my radio amateur licence qualification) but that did not succeed.

In October, I applied to the Civil Service for a post as an Executive Officer and was interviewed in London. One member of the interview panel asked about life in Thurso. I explained that I had been unemployed there, despite my physics degree, as Tom felt that as he was responsible for staffing he could not put his own son forward. A discussion about Highland unemployment resulted where one of the interview panel revealed that his brother worked in the Social Security office in Wick. This produced a mini-debate on unemployment in the Highlands. A week or two later came an offer of appointment to the Crofters Commission in Inverness, starting on 1 January 1973 (not possible as 1 and 2 January were public holidays in Scotland). From 3 January, I worked at the Commission, responsible for crofting in North Shetland and Orkney, an exciting time at the very start of the Shetland oil industry.

I was a novelty for the Commission; many of the staff had worked there since it opened in 1955, some straight from school and many of the working methods were of that era. There was

Reay Beach

a typing pool of ladies who would decipher manuscript draft letters and minutes and produce a paper version. There were no photocopiers so carbon paper copies were made by the typist or for those needing large numbers a stencil would be "cut" with which 30 copies could be made. No English person had worked there before and I was probably the youngest person in the whole office. The only other member of staff who had been to university was the Secretary to the Commission, Donald John McCuish. I worked with a Commissioner, Robert Bruce then Lord Lieutenant of Shetland. The Commission met monthly to which we had to report on our areas or present difficult cases for decision.

With the solid prospects of a civil service career, I was able to secure a mortgage and in June 1973 moved into a newly-built, two-bedroom, detached bungalow in Maryburgh, near Dingwall. This was a 20 mile drive from Inverness – an easy commute to a site overlooking the Conon Firth. In mid-August, Tom and Phyll drove from Lymm to Maryburgh to see the new house. It was a glorious, warm, sunny week and much time was spent exploring the area. On Saturday 18 August, Tom and I prepared and levelled the side garden for seeding a lawn; it was a bit hot for that but everyone was keen.

We could see the beaches of the River Conon and another new life (mine) was underway.

Reay Beach

Consequences

Tom died during the night.

He had a heart attack, the final consequence of the major surgery of a couple of years earlier. The surgery had been to remove an "idiopathic retro-peritoneal fibrosis". This diagnosis says the fibrosis was of unknown origin but it was clearly caused by radiation he had received in Australia just 20 years earlier. The doctors in Inverness had given Tom's condition a concocted name, probably to avoid making a connection to radiation – at that time Governments were still refusing to recognise what was happening. Phyll also refused to make this connection, outside the family and friends, as she recognised Tom had been a member of the team planning and delivering the Maralinga tests, at a time when little was known of the possible effects.

The Australian tests were conducted by two groups of people:

Those who knew:

what was being prepared and why. Sir William Penney, the British equivalent to, and who had worked closely with, the American Robert Oppenheimer. As the head of the British delegation working on the Manhattan Project at Los Alamos Laboratory, Penney initially carried out calculations to predict the damage effects generated by the blast wave of an atomic bomb. He was present at the dropping of the bomb on Nagasaki.

Consequences

The nuclear scientists also knew of the long term effects of radiation. Marie Curie, who discovered radium and polonium, won two Nobel prizes and had the unit of radioactivity, the curie, named after her. She died of aplastic anaemia believed to have been contracted from her long-term exposure to radiation, causing damage to her bone marrow. Everyone at Aldermaston knew the basics, most knew the detail.

Tom worked closely with Sir William Penney (knighted in 1952) who was to become Baron Penney of East Hendred in 1967, and received the Order of Merit in 1969.

A key figure was Len Beadell– a man of Australia entirely at home in the outback, a true Indiana Jones – who enabled the test sites to be identified, supplied and much more. His book "Blast the Bush" is modest about his role but without him the project might never have been completed.

Those who knew little:

who acted faithfully with discipline, under instructions. There were large numbers of people, primarily military, who were used to carrying out orders, without much questioning. They cleared ground, built runways, accommodation, workshops and laboratories, in very distant places like Monte Bello, Woomera and Maralinga, in Australia. The military could not function with much in the way of questioning orders.

This was how the atomic bomb was built and tested. The scene was complicated by the arrival of an enemy, that sought and gained secrets about what was being built and how. The rise of

Consequences

communism, especially the Stalin version, added another layer of complexity. In contrast, today's space exploration, every bit as difficult (perhaps more so) is conducted almost in public with its proponents leading rock star lives.

All this has produced a furore for compensation for those whose lives have been affected by the nuclear bomb tests. Virtually all open air testing ended by 1960 so nearly all those affected directly have died. When Tom died the clamour for compensation was only just starting. Phyll could easily have asked for some recognition; we discussed it and concluded that Tom had a fair idea of the risks. We decided not join the campaigns, which continue today – he had felt that he was doing his duty. In part that duty included making clear that the weapons which had been developed and stored should never, in fact, could never, be used. Without Hiroshima and Nagasaki, for all their horror, that war (and the next) might have continued for years, with an even greater number of casualties.

50 years later, the family applied for the British Nuclear Test Medal. It arrived in a plain envelope including a message:

> "in recognition of the significant contribution made by your loved one to Britain's nuclear test programme".

Neither the Medal nor the accompanying presentation note name the person for which it is awarded.

In contrast, the elegant medals Tom was awarded during the War and those of Phyll's ancestors, from the South African wars of 1901 and WW1 1914-18, do carry their names, rank and

Consequences

number. It might be said they were for battles and campaigns fought. Tom's "no name" medal is to mark a war put on hold.

In 1914, H.G. Wells produced his book "The War That Will End War" anticipating what was to come. That conflict and that of 1939-45 did not achieve that objective, at all, but a few men in American and Australian deserts deterred any further attempt to deliver security by guns and bombs.

In 2025, that taut and tense peace seems under threat.

It is always tempting to say "if only…"

For Tom and his family, the "if only…" would be that working on the atomic weapons project, seeing those astonishing weapons explode in 1956, led to an early death.

So what put him there?

"If only…" he had stayed in London doing a moderately tedious job in the Ministry of Supply he might not have gone to Glasgow where Phyll found things difficult.

"If only…" he had stayed at school and gone on to teacher training college, he might have stayed in the north – and would not have met Phyll.

"If only…" there had not been a war he might have become a barman in the Conservative Club in Sunderland.

"If only…" he had not… now this is the tricky one. Did Tom find out that James Edgar was not his father? Was it blurted out in some family row? It is easy to think (wrongly) that with two

Consequences

albino children there was a high risk of more and when that didn't turn out questions were asked. Or did Hannah reveal quietly and affectionately to her son that the secret liaison happened and he regarded that as a release for her and for him.

If only…" Thomas Taylor Ferry had not told someone what he and Hannah had done. In fact, no one may have been told. The DNA legacy revealed enough.

In truth… none of these parallel universes would have given Tom and his family lives which were as good as what actually did happen.

The Family Tree

The availability of cheap, reliable DNA testing has become the background to many stories of families with unknown members and secret liaisons. However, the research in families past received it first impetus from the arrival of the routine creation of a register of the whole population, in the censuses held in England every 10 year since 1841. As public documents, controlled by formally appointed registrars, they appear to be definitive. Science had little to do with it.

Two independent but interconnected ideas have changed much of this. Websites like Ancestry.co.uk and Find My Past have used sophisticated computer analysis to search millions of references suggest connections. However, they rely on the returns made by ordinary people and secrets can still be kept.

Nature keeps a record of its own. The instructions for assembling each and every plant, insect, fish, bird and animal are contained in every cell of their bodies – which contain a large molecule, called DNA which was finally understood in 1952. This carries the code for each of us.

I have tested my DNA (a saliva sample) with that of John Frederick Pearson; we've never met but we recognise ancestors we should have in common. The results show that he and I do not share male line DNA - there is no reason to doubt his line

The Family Tree

and every doubt about mine. He is descended from Miles Abstemious Pearson and I am not.

On Ancestry (the website), my DNA matched, quite closely, that of Alan Ferry. We agree that the father of my father, Thomas Wilfred Pearson, was Thomas Taylor Ferry, Alan's grandfather. This chart shows the years of birth of all concerned.

Thomas Wilfred Pearson was born on 8 September 1922.

Thomas Taylor Ferry (the 2nd) was born on 12 July 1923.

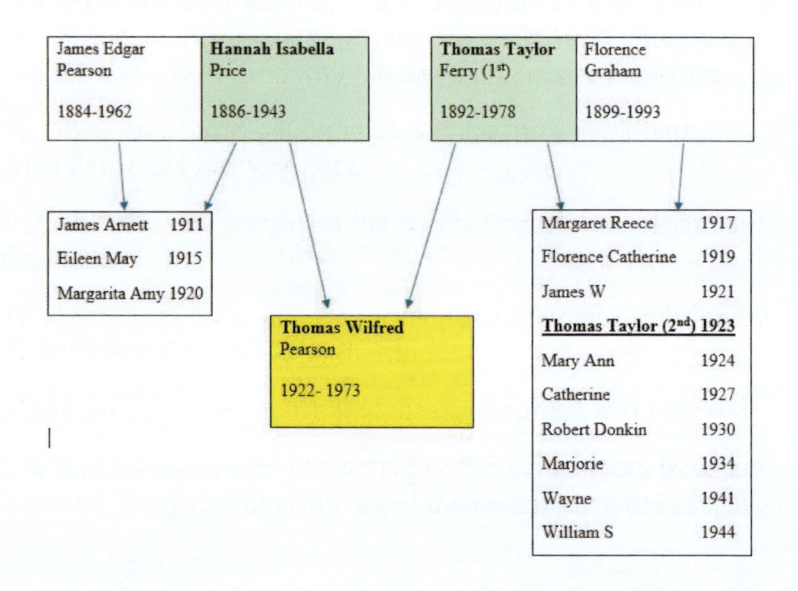

James Edgar Pearson	Hannah Isabella Price		Thomas Taylor Ferry (1st)	Florence Graham
1884-1962	1886-1943		1892-1978	1899-1993

James Arnett	1911
Eileen May	1915
Margarita Amy	1920

Thomas Wilfred Pearson
1922- 1973

Margaret Reece	1917
Florence Catherine	1919
James W	1921
Thomas Taylor (2nd)	**1923**
Mary Ann	1924
Catherine	1927
Robert Donkin	1930
Marjorie	1934
Wayne	1941
William S	1944

The Family Tree

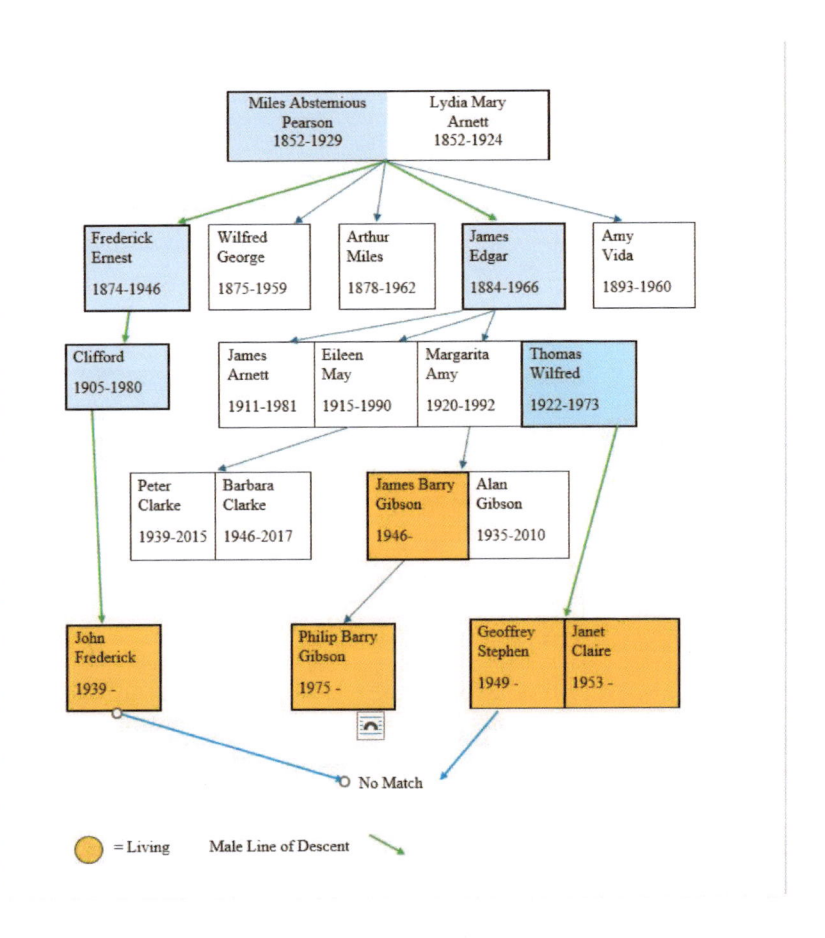

Miles Abstemious Pearson 1852-1929 — **Lydia Mary Arnett** 1852-1924

Children:
- **Frederick Ernest** 1874-1946
- **Wilfred George** 1875-1959
- **Arthur Miles** 1878-1962
- **James Edgar** 1884-1966
- **Amy Vida** 1893-1960

Frederick Ernest → **Clifford** 1905-1980

James Edgar's children: **James Arnett** 1911-1981 | **Eileen May** 1915-1990 | **Margarita Amy** 1920-1992 | **Thomas Wilfred** 1922-1973

Eileen May's children: **Peter Clarke** 1939-2015 | **Barbara Clarke** 1946-2017

Margarita Amy's children: **James Barry Gibson** 1946- | **Alan Gibson** 1935-2010

Clifford → **John Frederick** 1939 -

James Barry Gibson → **Philip Barry Gibson** 1975 -

Thomas Wilfred → **Geoffrey Stephen** 1949 - | **Janet Claire** 1953 -

John Frederick → No Match
Geoffrey Stephen → No Match

● = Living   Male Line of Descent →

171

Acknowledgements

All together this story has taken 25 years, peering into the past, decoding the few documents and relics which have survived over many decades. In this my sister, Jan Whitehead, has been a constant support and, importantly, had an alternative perspective and a much better memory. Even so, there are many gaps.

I am grateful to Richard Dawkins who responded with alacrity to my request for a DNA test and to my distant cousin, Phil Dawkins, who runs the Dawkins Genealogy website.

In assembling the material, I have welcomed the generous loan by my cousin, Peter Clarke, of his mother's 1932 photograph albums and advice from my cousin, Christopher Dawkins.

The final impetus to get on with it came from my kinsman, Alan Ferry and his wife Sara.

I've had valuable advice on the production process from Paul Chiswick.

The Maralinga paintings were brought into good condition by The Scottish Conservation Studio.

Many friends have contributed ideas, comment and material.

I've had relentless and patient support over 50 years from my husband, Tony Cairns, who urged me to complete the project.

Sources

The main source was the accumulated material which Tom and Phyll had assembled and retained: school report books, annotated text books, Army papers, wedding souvenirs and many items from Australia.

"The Story of the R.A.S.C, 1939-45" by the R.A.S.C. History Committee, published by The Naval and Military Press Ltd

"Britain, Australia and the bomb : the nuclear tests and their aftermath" Author: Arnold, Lorna.

The National Archives of Western Australia

The National Library of Scotland

Ancestry.co.uk

Findmypast.co.uk

FreeBMD.org.uk

Family papers

Sources

The Beadell family archive has been most helpful. Len Beadell's book on the British bomb tests has been republished.

https://www.lenbeadell.com./

About the Author

Geoff Pearson thought, in part because of Tom's experience, that he wished to be a physicist but, as Roker Beach relates, that plan changed. Instead he became a civil servant in the Scottish Office and later the Scottish Government, from 1973 to retirement in 2011, working on everything from the Icelandic Cod War to the National Health Service.

A good part of that time was spent supporting Ministers in taking legislation through the UK Houses of Parliament and the Scottish Parliament and writing speeches for others to deliver. In retirement he has had various roles in the third sector.

The story is for Joss and Phoebe Whitehead and Betty Thorpe.

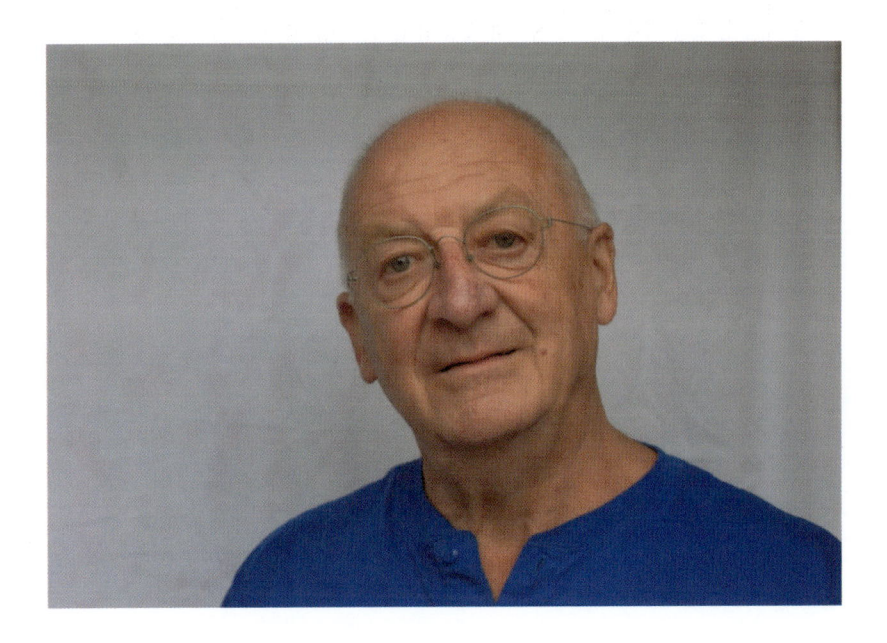

Printed in Great Britain
by Amazon